A Million and
More Strides

E. HECTOR KYME

A Million and More Strides

Photographs by the author

ROBERT HALE · LONDON

First published in Great Britain 1975

ISBN 0 7091 4754 6

Robert Hale & Company
63 Old Brompton Road
London SW7

To/ My Darling Wife,
Easter 1975.
Alan.

Printed in Great Britain by
Northumberland Press Limited
and bound by Richard Clay (The Chaucer Press) Limited,
Bungay, Suffolk

Contents

Illustrations

Acknowledgements

IT WOULD be a tremendous list of people were I to mention all the fine folk who made this 800-mile walk possible, but to some I must make special reference. They are the numerous people, who, without notice in many cases, opened up their rooms at great inconvenience to give me comfortable accommodation, and provide fine meals, also added to which, the inevitable food and drink needed for the next leg of the journey.

These good Samaritans, both men and women, included hoteliers, inn-keepers, boarding-house keepers, youth hostel wardens, farmers, school-teachers and caretakers, ministers of religion, postmen, musicians, and that fine company of ordinary householders who gave me fantastic welcome to their hearths.

Equally important to the success of the venture and without whose co-operation I would not have contemplated starting out were the telephone operators. Particularly in the north of Scotland, their cheery voices often assured me Dronfield would soon be linked up so that my wife and I could have our evening chat.

To my two great friends, Roger A. Redfern the distinguished author, rambler and climber, and Frank Hepworth a fanatical walker and naturalist, I owe a great debt of gratitude for their kindness in taking me into Scotland, the wild Pennines and Peak District, and the softer character of Derbyshire and Nottinghamshire. With these stalwarts I received much of the needful experience to grapple with violent extremes of weather and terrain, with the added thrill of obtaining photographs in wild unspoilt country.

To Mrs Judith Mills my typist who has miraculously interpreted my scrawl, and who has worked relentlessly with great enthusiasm, I owe very grateful thanks.

Also to the publishers Robert Hale and Co., through their editor G. Chesterfield, I owe much gratitude for kindly and helpful criticism and encouragement to complete this tremendous pictorial jigsaw puzzle of words.

Lastly, to the one who over many years has walked and waited with me to obtain photographs often in difficult places, even for people many years her junior, I owe my greatest tribute of praise. Her preparations for my walks are done with loving care and patience—though she has a fault: she once had me carry seventeen handkerchiefs! To pay her recognition which will obviously be unbiased, being from one acquaintance, I quote the words of a Welsh farmer's wife, who had asked how far she had walked with me on a day's stroll in Anglesey. The woman said "She's marvellous!" I heartily agree with the statement. I ought to, for she's Dora my wife.

Dronfield E. Hector Kyme

I *On Top of Britain—* *On Top of the World*

WITH one elbow resting on the roof of his superb car, affording support while divesting himself of his fishing waders, an angler answered my "How do you do?" with "Good day, where are you going?"

"Dover, sir," I said casually.

"Say that again?" he retorted.

"Dover sir, walking all the way."

"Good heavens man, are you serious?"

As I assured him, he attracted his wife's attention from her reading in the car's sumptuous upholstery, and she then expressed equal amazement regarding my project.

"Have a tot of this," he said as he produced a hip flask from his pocket.

"Teetotal, thanks all the same."

"Bother that, it will do you good, you'll need it," he said. Then, as he saw my camera, he asked if I would photograph his catch of two salmon. His wife inferred I had plenty of other more important things pending for my photographic prowess and tried to dissuade me from fulfilling his request. On lifting the boot flap, I saw two beauties and completed Perry Aldworth's field-day by photographing him supporting them in his firm grasp, providing a permanent reminder of that unique occasion of his success.

Yes, but all this happened in a little layby, a passing place some six miles south of Durness, where I was apprehensive and eager to press on without hindrance, as I had fourteen miles to cover to reach Rhiconich, carrying a thirty-pound pack, and honour bound to accept no lifts.

I had made a start, but to 'begin', as Alice said, at the 'beginning' here goes:

My plan had been ruined at the intended start, as foul weather prevented access to Cape Wrath—the very tip of north-west Scotland, the ferry boat being unavailable for two days. For a whole day a savage wind hacked at the Kyle's treacherous water as I mouched in its vicinity and the ferry-man could not be induced to take me over the rollicking waves. Dejectedly I carried my pack to the very edge of the high cliffs and watched the prancing sea-horses right out towards Cape Wrath which could just be seen and then 'set off', but only to the village of Durness.

From Faraid Head I left the sight of boiling surf far below 329 feet down and thought NOW FOR DOVER, not without a prayer in my heart in thankfulness and confidence. Casting a glance to the far north-west, I could see Cape Wrath's prominence of 500 feet terminating the north coast's savage rocks and over all a glorious sky with flotillas of billowy clouds edged in gold by a 'back-lit' sun. A fellow unknown to me, curious about my load, asked if he could join me as I sauntered down the long expanse of cropped grass amongst and through the chummy groups of cattle and sheep, which grazed in contentment above the bay and sand dunes.

Arthur Bunn, a veteran motor cyclist, proceeded ahead as we reached the sublimest bay one sees in a lifetime, while I dipped a hand in the sea indicating 'I've been here' and then caught him up. We circuited the shining, restless waters of Balnakeil Bay, seen by another couple intent on seeking shells. I'm glad I saw Balnakeil the night before at the sun's down—alone—there was no one else. The roar of wind and waves reminded me of Mendelssohn's 'Fingal's Cave' as the sea-horses raced towards me with their manes flung back in the fast-flying spume from an opposing wind. Dry sand, clean, swept along like drifting snow adding to the huge dunes topped with lashing grass. Dunlins pattered along the edges of runnels in the shallows careless of my approach—what had they to fear? It seemed that it must have been a million years ago, unspoilt by man.

There is one old house and a ruined church which guards the scene where the elements ring the changes of sunshine, hissing rain and whining wind; these look out towards the

1216 feet Sgribhis in an evening, with its cloudy mane framing its beauty, and beyond all is wildness to the Cape. Balnakeil is grandeur always in the making, seasons in and out, days and nights under sun or moon—it is ever new, God in creation. I look forward one day, to racing barefooted across the sands, into the shallows left by receding waves, to add yet another enchantment to the memory.

Arthur continued with me to Durness, turning our backs on this fantastic shore and leaving the two shell-gatherers unaware the bay was theirs alone.

The narrow lane bordered by low stone walls fenced in a few fields which yielded crops of hay—cattle fodder—being gathered by bare-armed farmers using a tractor and waggon. An off-shoot lane led to squat army-type hutments now used as busy craft houses by artists and weavers, who are a craft community living away from the towns. We were soon passing the first ruined house near the village with its stout skeleton of massive stones with corner quoins, gable-built into the wind, not face-side on. The old chimney, spacious to allow the exit of peat smoke, still stood defiantly against any weather. Old sods and thatch still cling to the bulky untrimmed timbers, still a miracle of craftsmanship that any trace be left after hurricane-force winds. No more will its earth floor be used or tolerated, nor will its low doorway ever again admit the stocky, bearded highlander. Long may it remain as such a reminder of grim days when men lived by use of brain and sinew and not be taken over for rebuilding as a modern holiday home.

Back to the village wandering amongst the Snowcemmed bungalows, festooned with wires for telephone or electric supply and hereabouts a Calor gas cylinder; modernism has taken Durness by storm and made the lives of the warm-hearted folk much easier. Two men rebuild a broken wall on a bend. They work hard, have to, to keep warm, but they are interested in their task and assemble the rough stones into a beautiful wall that 'looks right' to the eye, for no lines or templates are used. Because I was interested they exchanged a few words, but kept on working.

A retired lighthouse-keeper from Cape Wrath, now serving as local information officer from his snug, tidy caravan office, advised me what to 'see' and taking note I went to the eastern edge of the straggly village to Smoo cave. It has a haunting beauty, and long ago was the burial place of notables. Before leaving the road, look landwards over the bridge and you will see a stream, look over the other, the seaward side, and the stream has disappeared—*where?* We descend into the ravine, warily across stepping-stones, into the cavernous hole deep and gloomy with eerie light from 'heaven'—a hole in the roof. A roar indicates falling water at the back of the cave: of course, the emergence of the 'lost' stream which flows into the nearby sea.

Clambering up the winding path and wending up and down steeply to Mrs Mather's grocer's shop along the most northerly road, my bag was stocked with all likely necessary items for my next day's fourteen miles' journey, where she crammed in extras for nothing out of goodwill.

At 7 a.m. I left the dormitory, crossed the wildly wet-open-draughty twenty yards' space to the dining-room where I knew I would be alone and able to make unhindered preparations for departure.

Soon I was ready, when Woods, the hostel wardens—my friends—and a few people wished me well and desired a card from Dover—they knew I'd do it! The post mistress told me to address one to myself from Durness and another from Dover—"Send me one please mister"—which I did—later. I felt it a great challenge at sixty-five carrying thirty pounds all the way to Rhiconich, fourteen miles, having only practised six-mile stints over the last month. The weight steadied me in the boisterous wind, which blew my stick across the front of me if I didn't consciously control it. The drizzle was uncomfortable but cooling, and partially obliterated my view of the last remote dwelling, the Cape Wrath Hotel, which disappeared altogether as I progressed alongside the savage Kyle of Durness. Here it was thrilling to have the open road to myself, which was fenceless and wide open to the moorland and massive mountains, haunts of the wild stag, scene of the brawling stream and fierce cataract, canopied by pure blue and scudding fretted clouds, the wild haunts of hardy black-faced sheep which weaker breeds would never endure. Here at long last was I satisfying the aboriginal in me—fending for myself independent of time or distance, able to stand and stare, unfettered—*free!*

Out here one can see to the north high rolling contours over a thousand feet and left, thrilling shapes shutting off the southwards with 2000 feet mountains. The sheep wander freely across the road and suckle their lambs now almost as large as themselves. But, my load needs adjustment, the sun breaks through and the shepherd's house is a good place for local lore while I'm packing away my drying anorak. Martin Mackay and his wife will receive us gladly and their two young sons will see if we can whistle with our fingers.

Shepherd Mackay and his wife told me of one hazardous journey made shepherding when a number of men with vehicles went to Cape Wrath ferry to be left there until evening, when the men, having done their work, would use them to return again. After a tiring day, on reaching the landing they found the ferry crossing too dangerous to negotiate and consequently were obliged to walk round through bogs, over the wild area around the loch. The six-mile trudge continued in the dark across burns and mire until they reached the road, which still had to be walked to their homes. Their anxious wives dare not think what disaster may have overtaken them and could only watch and wait, having the fire bright and the kettles steaming if and when their men returned.

I left the cottage as Martin with his sprained ankle came to the door with his wife and boys; grateful for the cup of tea and Scotch cake I was soon into my stride with the sun and clouds, magnificent deep colouring under the cloud shadows enhanced the brilliance of verdure, still wet, in the glorious blaze of light. I felt like Moses, who removed his shoes when he heard, "The place whereon thou standest is holy ground". This gorgeous panorama seemed like the robe of God. The ground, boulder-strewn in the River Dionard with greens and browns glistening with sodden grass and rushes, seemed like a regal carpet. Higher and steeper to the heavens, cropped grasses, fringed with the white ermine of cascading streams, was as the very garment itself. Atop of this tremendous scene where mountain-tops pierced the glowing clouds into the blue of a perfect sky was sublimity itself.

I realized more than ever happiness is not bought and found I was forgetting my pack in spite of the climb.

I rummaged for a snack after picking a suitable rock to sit on and looking north-west thought of the Cape Wrath lighthouse-keeper with his family out yonder, devotees to the cause of safer shipping; surely they enjoy the wildness of nature as I did myself. But enough with ruminating, up and off I started, the only walker on the long, long, steep climb. The few motorists would wave a hand or give a toot and others offer me a lift (seventy-five of them kindly extending their goodwill in the full length of my journey).

Scrutinizing my map I felt satisfaction as good mileage was being made and feeling fit, with determination I struck out to finishing the climb for an easier four miles descent. After six miles, in a lonely spot above the brawling Dionard, a posh car stood in a fisherman's layby. Two rods lay on the roof just clear of an elbow supporting a fellow removing his waders. His deerstalker hat and sophisticated outfit indicated an enthusiast, but his actions suggested he had finished his angling for that day, at least. I spoke, to which he replied, "Good day, where are you going?" "Dover, sir." Of course he was Perry Aldworth from Kent who had caught two salmon that morning. Worth the journey? A thousand times!

We parted, myself to sweat and toil up the incline, until reaching a cascade of water running into a large horse trough with a notice adjacent and read: *"1883 of gratitude and respect to the Inhabitants of Durness and Eddrachillis for their hospitality while projecting this road. This inscription is placed over this well by their humble servant. Peter Lawson. Surveyor."* This former road engineer experienced the same fine hospitality as I later did throughout the highlands. I drank and like a giant refreshed raced on—I was told later the water mixes well with whisky to make the journey tolerable if not enjoyable, yet I resolved 'soberly' to continue, keeping to the right of the road until my first good Samaritans, the Vernons from Surrey, offered me a lift. "No, I must walk all the distance except where there are ferries."

A long slog eventually brought me to the summit where with no one, not a living thing in sight, acute loneliness shook me as I looked ahead. There into the tremendous distance, four ranges of mountains went into recession indicating the far-reaching journey and beyond, and only now begun. This is no time to think of the difficulties ahead, press on, I thought, as between eerie rock formations and moors I tramped, when a solitary van came and went and then returned, the old man driving telling me Rhiconich was only 1½ miles distant. "A lift?" I told him my project which pleased him as he let in his clutch and gently 'purred' away to the village. You'll do it young man—14 miles! ! I said to myself, and felt one of life's richest experiences reaching fulfilment, for there, round a bend on a hillside in the evening light, were four cottages—*Rhiconich*. Never were houses —*homes*—quite like this to me before.

My way now passed beyond a bridge over the river running into Loch Inchard, where I looked landwards to the great mountains Foinaven and Arkle, 2580 feet rearing skywards and superbly dominating this wonderful Sutherland landscape. Soon after, with a grand meal before me provided by Mrs William Falconer, I learned from her postman husband that the Duchess of Westminster names all her race horses after the mountains on her estate in the locality, and Arkle, as even laymen know, was one of the greatest horses of all time; well he should have been, named after such a majestic mountain.

It felt great to be on top of Britain; I was on top of the world.

2 *Serene Silence*

William and Ina Falconer's home was a two-storeyed dwelling-house, probably modernized on the old foundation of a former cottage; they had every modern facility, a hot bath being ready for me in minutes of my arrival.

Willie was proud of his appearance on TV about the work of a highland postman and showed me his photograph. Although both he and his wife—who keeps the post office—are near retirement, they are remarkably fit, for Willie goes a daily journey of eleven miles over rough country in all weathers, delivering postal packages, medicines, papers, packages from one house to another and nice gossip. He is a friend of all and enemy of none. Of course he's a travelling news agency, passing messages from house to house and many's the cup o'tea ready for when he crosses a threshold.

I questioned Ina and Willie about my apartments at Scourie and the time it would take me to do twelve miles; he lifted my rucksack as if it were filled with feathers and then estimated half the hours it took me later.

While recounting the community life of the district, they spoke of the visitation of migrant evangelists and colporteurs, folk being eager to live in close harmony with God.

At one of a few occasions when removing my handkerchief, a coin rolled on the floor. Investigations revealed a hole in my purse. I wished to repair the defect myself but they refused to allow me, and Willie, doffing his double thick glasses for the short-sighted, soon had needle and thread plying, but I only received it when Ina had cast a critical eye to 'see if it would do'.

After a fine rest and refreshment this grand couple saw me off on a Sunday morning into the eerie land around Rhiconich, where massive rocks thrust through the rough earth and mosses, grasses, brackens and rushes crowd on each other for possession of the peaty or gritty ground. Pools of every size and shape fill the hollows, some so large as to warrant a name, completing an uttermost loneliness in amongst the land masses as I trudged on and on along the twisting road, and being Sunday I recall only four cars passing me in twelve miles. 'A peace which knows no understanding' gripped me as never before.

Nearing Laxford Bridge there are hillsides with south-west aspects towards the sun which bear traces of cultivation and crofting, with long rows of stones separating the strips of land. Sporadically situated are mounds of stones, once the poor hovels of crofters who with their families eked a living from the few oats grown, or from the few beast and sheep reared on their land. Covetous lairds desired more territory for pasturage in the time of the 'Clearances' and hired thugs to demolish the homes of the distraught crofters, leaving them to wander until they could be adopted by another society or be sent abroad.

It is not all grim, for having reached Laxford Bridge with its stretch of water out to sea like some fine lagoon, I sat down at a picnic bench and joined in with two other folk for lunch. We found serenity from the maddening rush amongst the sheltering mountains in the warm sunshine and gentle wind; no wonder, we agreed, that the Royal Family sail around the shores of the north-west, and Prince Charles does his fishing near the bridge. The two nurses went northwards as I left, passing two solitary houses and then the bridge, where after a moment's watching I saw a huge salmon leap in the fierce waters and disappear in the torrent.

A nostalgic twinge gripped me at the road junction for Inverness and the 'train for home', but straightway I turned westwards by a huge coniferous plantation, and strode out along the straight, modernized double-width road. It could have well been in the backwoods of Canada and well might a huge grizzly bear have emerged from the dark gloom of thick-set trunks.

A steady rhythmic plod and my burning thirst were conducive to slumber and I felt that I would see no one for another five miles at least, when suddenly in a small clearing four forestry houses revealed themselves. By a neatly clipped hedge stood a man whom I approached for a drink, when our voices stirred the quiet afternoon to life. His wife, having heard my request, had me enter their best room, supplying me with tea, scones, jam, after I'd feasted on fresh salmon and salad. Who said the Scots are mean? Mrs John Mackenzie asked, "Where are you staying at Scourie?"

"Mrs Norman Macleod's Rowan Lodge."

"Och, that's our daughter's. We'll take you in the car."

"Thanks indeed, but *I'm walking*."

"Och, yes, so you said—but let us take your rucksack."

"Sorry, must carry that all the way also."

John Mackenzie is a forestry foreman on the Duchess of Westminster's estate and looking into the distance of that vast panorama I envied him his job which takes him amongst those great uplands. I warmly thanked my unexpected hosts, who then proceeded ahead to herald my coming, while I followed in the balmy air sauntering on the road and looking at the changing mountain contours. Foinaven and Arkle had a warm pinkish glow with lower slopes of gorgeous greens and browns like Skiddaw of the English Lake District. I kept turning round and contemplating Ben Stack, 2364 feet high, as finely proportioned as the great Matterhorn; Scotland hereabouts possesses the notable features of so many other lands, Canada, England, Switzerland, and the wild coastline next the restless sea.

Of all the mountain guardians of lochs, I know of no finer sight than of Ben Stack, which stands over the loch of the same name brooding like a conquering giant with the 'racing steeds' on the opposite flanks. My first ever sight of these fearsome heights was on a rainy evening gloomy and forbidding, when I saw a boat containing four dour anglers accoutred with waterproofs and sou'westers—more than a match for wildest weather. These men, enjoying themselves in such foul conditions, contributed to my resolution in similar bad weather—and worse—to make scheduled progress.

Now still under the high sun, I forged on between the wilderness of rocks and heather separated from the nearby sea, to be startled by a man and woman 'roughing it' on the wild moor which they left to escort me into the village of Scourie. This I found contained both old and modern dwellings neat and trim with walls and fences to pleasant gardens, where I had no difficulty in finding Rowan Lodge.

3 *A Million and More Strides*

Mrs Macleod, aware of my coming from her parents' information, had a nice meal for me and having dined I went round the village. The Gulf Stream's warmth affects the climate, so that some huge sycamores grew in a sheltered quarter, together with some sweet chestnuts and two palm trees. A rich greenness gave way to yellow grass stubble, where late hay had not long been gathered, and hens wandered about, around the out-buildings, and even the doorways of the cottages. Shippons were tidy with concrete floors for easy cleaning and a general efficiency pervaded the whole village.

The war memorial well tended, surrounded by good property, indicated signs of general prosperity. The sea curving in from the north-west, sheltered by rising ground, was near enough from any part of the village for a mother carrying a bairn and bringing a toddler to wander down to the shore to take a respite from her chores. It was very quiet as darkness came—no sound of transistors or automobiles, no shrieking children—(they had gone to bed)—and with an autumn bank holiday due in the morning, Norman and his wife could afford an extra hour to talk with me about the locality.

In 1951 a horrifying gale terrified the local people as it smashed property and wrenched branches from the trees, driving the folk into their stout, strong-walled coal houses until it abated.

"What happens when an aspirin won't solve the trouble? Have you a resident doctor?"

"Och, yes, and the dentist visits the district monthly. As for a hospital case, the patient is taken or fetched to the hospital at Golspie on the east coast, some sixty miles."

Since there are no mechanical industries, the menfolk run a croft with a few cows, sheep and poultry, while taking on other jobs like council work, such as road-mending, or

-making, wall-building, fence erections, or maybe run a lobster fishing boat. A keen man will farm six cows and fifty sheep and sell them at auctions forty miles away, thus able to settle his rent payment.

I had observed in places two or three cottages would be built a few hundred yards apart and wondered if there was a 'free masonry' between the inhabitants. "Och yes, householders usually meet neighbours some part of the day to exchange news good or bad and to give maybe a helping hand."

A former veterinary surgeon told me that not long ago, in the north-west, farmers would tie a piece of red ribbon round each cow's tail to ward off the evils of the Devil, and place over the inside door lintel a shelf to contain an open Bible to avoid the same evil spells entering their homes. There are some folk who readily accept it a wise precaution to grow a rowan tree near the house even in these days. To have one will bring good luck, to damage one in any way will court disaster.

Supper and then bed—had me as fit as a fiddle for Kylesku Ferry the next day, when Norman and his wife saw me away well stocked with food for the journey. In fact Norman took me a 'short cut', up a steep field to have a chat with an old and respected resident of Scourie.

Flossie the old sheep dog heralded our approach to the farm clean as a new pin. Then we passed the peat pile built with the pride of a craftsman, between the clucking hens and finally to the door where I was introduced to a refined, retired gentleman.

The old man informed me about current schooling in the village where approximately twenty pupils attend the primary school until reaching the age of eleven or twelve, then real adventure begins when boarding at a secondary modern school at Golspie. Coming home after a 'term' is a realistic holiday, and on occasion the children have a long weekend with their parents. Being away from Mum and Dad and living with others encourages good manners and better sociability, as I found later.

I left my informant, with a view to commencing my eleven miles to Kylesku the next village, regarding the undertaking contemptuously—A mere eleven miles, *easy!* I was to be greatly disillusioned, for it was noon turned before really starting off. Having climbed the hill field, the view back was fine, and 'going' was easy—and having left Flossie seeing me away from one homestead, a golden labrador met me when approaching another. He led me, tail wagging, to a large wooden shed smelling strongly of oak and pine shavings, where reared up outside the building were strong lobster boats suitable for rowing or for outboard motors and inside a boat in progress lay upon two trestles. I was startled when a voice from a man I hadn't noticed addressed me politely and hearing of my interest in his work, began to describe his daily routine. He was a kindly, wiry, sixtyish man who scanned me over his glasses. A more contented fellow you won't find; for ever sawing, planing, boring, spokeshaving, pitching, tarring and painting—a proud craftsman making boats he dare sail himself. Self-taught, Robert Mackiness, sixty-two, builds clinker boats from larch and oak and enjoys the intricacies of steam bending; and particularly likes the facilities provided by electric power: it is a delight for him drilling each hole carefully with a modern contraption—an electric drill.

Robert added—electricity has proved a boon to all, for washing machines, fridges, TV and 'fires', but for him personally the circular saw has taken the drudgery out of his labour. This man who has no union troubles, does need the help of another when riveting where he can't reach both sides, then someone holds the clenching hammer while he domes the rivet.

I left Robert Mackiness with his dog by his side in the shavings and went into the fierce sunlight, soon climbing to the highest limits of the village on the very twisting road, turned a corner and soon it was gone.

Fierce heat of over eighty degrees sweltered me in a natural oven between the high hills all around, the sea occasionally seen quite near when a little gap appeared on the seaward side. Round and about twisting and undulating fiercely steep, the road went amongst fine scenery, wild and majestic. A superb inland loch deep in a hollow had, distantly, three people by its shore a quarter of a mile away. I wondered if they would hear a finger whistle: they did, in this natural amphitheatre. I knew they had forgiven me breaking the silence, when they spoke, asking who I was—two Germans and one English, young ladies. "Are you married?" "Vat ist your first name?" "Hector." "Den your vife ist called Andromace ist she?" We nattered briefly and parted with *"auf Wiedersehen."*

To have carried sufficient one inch to the mile maps for my whole journey would have added bulk to the pack and two pounds extra weight, so making manage with a quarter-inch map where I knew direction, no indication was given of altitude changes and many were severely steep 'bottom gear' work. No sooner was one difficult stretch over, than there would be another round a mountain shoulder.

At last a grand glimpse of the sea and down almost to its edge, I gathered a few blackberries overhanging the rough sea wall at Badcall Bay. It was sublime, for the shining sea right out to the horizon couldn't be separated from the yellow-blue of the sky. There are here a dozen diminutive islands—little territories for sea birds, they seemed like lazy tortoises basking there in the autumn afternoon. Even the sea shared the serenity, for there was not one ripple, not a sound from earth or heaven that would disturb the 'tortoises' slumber.

A cottage 'slept' on the shore hillside overlooked by a derelict herring factory, long disused. A tea towel lazily wafted on a clothes-line and dried out as I ate my lunch—coffee all gone in *sweat*. It was when I needed water that the house awoke, the lady therefrom taking in the towel saw and waved to me, giving me the drink and topping up my flask. We parted, never to see each other again, so we thought. Although Mrs Weir said I could gladly stay at the farm when passing through Kent, where she really belonged.

I left the grassy patch in the dying heather and turned my back on the sleepy isles to climb the hill leading to the most toilsome journey of my life. Though Snowdon, Carrauntoohil, (3414 feet) Helvellyn and Clisham were heights I had previously climbed they were incomparable in effort required as was this Herculean task on a scorching day was the hardest prolonged physical feat of my life. There is no 'dropping in' at a café or shop en route, but simply to keep slogging it out until Kylesku Ferry is sighted.

The scenery became thrilling, range after range of mountains, with gorges and hollows through which the road passed. An impatient motorist sounded his hooter at every blind corner and broke the exquisite silence. Then a cyclist —the first I had seen—came steadily towards the north. He seemed glad for a word and scarcely had he gone when the colporteur I had seen previously hailed me from his van. "A lift? Of course, you are walking. Goodbye, all the best", and there in the wilderness of Sutherland I strove on alone.

Each ridge, each step a physical effort, the perspiration pouring from me—henceforth *sweat* would best describe the beads that ran into my eyes, salty and smarting. But, who are these? Two ill-clad men, glum, sweating like myself, father and son. It would seem, from the dilapidated field-glasses case the younger man carried, they were shepherds who had been searching for stray sheep. The senior grunted a demand for continuance of their journey as the younger wanted a chat with me, and in moments they and I were separated by the wild, forbidding rocky shoulders.

A narrowest of sea inlets appeared, only a stone's throw across, the rocky gorge scene of timeless storms and waves attacking the inundated coastline whose nearest match is like the Cornish coves.

Here at Rubh-a-Mhucard where there is barely room for a motor vehicle to negotiate the narrow road, I sought the cooling stream that chattered down the side of the steep ravine and threw the cold water over my head—showers and showers of the precious fluid. Then I drank and never was a giant more refreshed. As usual every hour, I had my target 'winner', a biscuit or a sandwich, and then continued. But here like the steep of Jacob's ladder, every single pace a challenge to continue, I guessed I had reached halfway to Kylesku. Let me see, I thought to offset the strain of striving, 800 miles times 1760, of course that's much more than a million paces. That's it, *A million and more strides*, the book title. Rounding a bend, high overlooking the sea, were four charming folk completely taken by surprise anyone should be walking. "Where are you going?" Being informed, they demanded I sat down to share their good companionship and the magnificent view.

It was here, the highest land I had encountered on this stretch, that was glorious indeed, for only four miles distant the fine mountain Quinag, 2653 feet, stretched out two prominences like the lying of a king and queen in state, under a cathedral roof of a brassy sky; 'they' seemed to be in eternal peace. Down again almost to sea level into a huge bowl through which a stream wandered in rocky terrain to the sea, then up again amongst pine plantations which make use of the wild land, for what animals can really thrive in such a country? Shepherding is often dangerous in mists and wild weather in Sutherland hence more attention is being given to afforestation in the county.

A small loch, dark and sinister, brooded down on the landward side, its calm surface occasionally stirred with silver rings from surfacing fish after flies. Some folk having watched and 'not carrying their pack' had left evidence 'they had been'—I pushed their broken fruit plates out of sight as I was too tired to take their refuse elsewhere, and continued in the evening glow of a perfect day. I asked a kindly motorist how far Kylesku was, and soon after I had quenched my thirst with his proffered lemon barley, my weary legs took me fast down past a farm, noisy with happy children.

It had been noticeable how observation of things on my walk had grown into a more acute discernment and keener memorization, perhaps from lack of human companionship—but here it was, perhaps out of sheer gratitude, after a broiling day, underestimating the severity of the journey, I recall an immaculate bottle-green car. Driven by a lady in a bottle-green dress, it stopped, on a narrow road where plantains and grasses grew in the middle of the main thoroughfare, to courteously offer me transport.

I could not accept her offer, but the fact someone cared in this instance gave me a 'red carpet' to walk the last remaining stretch. (I wish I had noted her address, I would have sent her a photograph of some aspect of the journey.)

The lady went ahead, soon lost beyond some fine trees which sheltered a few scattered houses. For what reason they were there puzzled me, but when I passed beyond them I beheld one of the grandest sights I have ever seen—the monster Quinag again. There in the afterglow of evening, the glassy waters of Loch Cairn Bawn stretched out, bordered by gloomy banks now devoid of sun, like some great castle courtyard and the giant Quinag guarding it. In the proximity of this 2653-foot mass glowering down, I felt 'cut down to scale' in God's eternity. It is well this scene comes as a suprise—for coming southwards, the hill masses prevent the viewing of the higher mountain; this panorama is one of the finest of Britain to me. The houses in the trees are probably connected with the open ferry running and maintenance crews, and their families, since a large shed stood dimly by the loch shore.

A final effort took me towards the ferry almost within hailing distance, and knowing it ceased at dusk, I began to run as fast as possible. Even so, there on my right a fine stag's head silhouetted, showed magnificently and near me. Information later told me he was in a compound, but what a sight as he lay near the water's edge. The ferrymen, seeing my hurry, 'thumbed me down' and as I boarded and crammed between the cars, strong hands grasped mine welcoming the 'man with red stockings and cap', for the crew had been told I was coming. It was one of life's proudest moments and I thanked God in my heart. It was a delight to receive the acclaim of the folk gathered around, and to fend off the almost bursting tears. I joined in kicking a large football up the slipway where two lads enjoyed the fun.

"Gentlemen, can you tell me of good accommodation please?" And soon I was received into Mrs Campbell's bungalow, where I fared like a prince; thereafter a rest and, after phoning home, to bed—serene in silence.

4 *By Miles and Feet to Inchnadamph*

On 'showing a leg' next morning, I was told by Mrs Campbell with two visitors, Harry and Dylis Owen, that a different programme for myself had been arranged, other than my own plan. Harry and Dylis were to take me a car run before I continued my marathon. "Och no," I said, "walk first relax afterwards." All were adamant. The next village being only ten miles away, I could easily manage that distance after our return and it would be impossible for me to do the distance to the second village another ten miles further ahead, so by a unanimous 'parliamentary' decision, I would go a car run; it would do me good "only I must be back by 2.30 at the latest".

Food packed, the Owens and I set off to see an extra portion of the coastline round by Drumbeg, Clashnessie, Lochinver to Inchnadamph, returning to Kylesku. Their kindness provided me with stupendous thrills of mountains and little bays, of crofts and crofters cutting late hay, their dogs following the machines, or riding on the empty hay carts. The very outset on this glorious morning showed Loch Glencoul shimmering like liquid silver, too dazzling to look upon, with the old school silhouetted and silent by its shore; and finally over Quinag, the fantastic Loch Assynt—of fresh water—revealed its little school also, merry with laughing children romping on the water's edge.

We were back late—very late—and by the time farewells were said to everyone, it was 4.15 before I resumed walking. However, before leaving, the accumulation of notes I took about the place and people provided facts of interest. The ferry is a 'free' one, since there is no other means for road transport to get further north, and Walter Brauer, a German widower, still so loves the area he stays as head ferryman, aided by Roddy Macleod and Colin Macleory. One of these only helps in the busy holiday season, otherwise he works for the County Council and runs his own croft. A young couple who had seen me arrive the night before fervently wished me success and good going.

I was introduced to old Mrs Moffat, a widow like her daughter Mrs Campbell, who had run the local hotel and now had this particular bungalow and annex for boarding holiday-makers.

Mrs Campbell had packed good food for me and filled my flask as Harry and Dylis filmed 'the departure' and I was 'off', turning occasionally to wave—they looked until I couldn't see them.

The steady but steep climb up the flanks of Quinag provided superb scenes, obtainable only by sweating as if in a Turkish bath. The sun directly ahead shining in my eyes gave me the excuses I wanted to turn round and look at the views. From my position, now high up, could be seen the little place occupied by the crofter, ferryman at Newton, then far away the mountain country of yesterday; then again I would turn to the task, mopping my brows with frequency.

After a wash in the stream and then my meal, the sun had slipped over the magnificent summit with its fierce glow still as burnished brass, making walking in the cool breeze down the ravine pleasurable indeed. The road between Kylesku and Loch Assynt is an engineering achievement skilfully easing the steepest gradients with steady climbs to 800 feet from either side of the mountain, I was near the top, 'monarch of all I surveyed', with the sublimest feeling of awe at such a wild and colossal landscape. I did not stop until down far below—four miles—I could see little Inchnadamph with its church, school, hotel and few cottages—one of which already had arranged for my coming.

My mind now easy, I sat to watch the glowing landscape for the sun had reappeared over Loch Assynt open to its light through the gap in the mountains. I then decided to race on to try and capture a sunset scene over the water. Whilst sitting, the smallest of objects moved almost imperceptibly over the landscape gradually coming towards me, until, churning away up the steep incline, a van with an elderly driver passed me—the same vehicle returning as I had started racing down the winding road. The man stopped, asking me to have a lift, being surprised at my refusal until he understood, and then he left and all was still. It seemed as silent as would be the Sahara, nothing moving save the setting golden orb over Loch Assynt and all I needed for my photograph was a foreground bush, tree or figure. At last as the gold had turned to red, a windswept tree struggling out of the sparse rocky ground afforded what I wanted as the camera clicked, with the sun touching the watery horizon—almost gone!

This, too, had been another great day and now with the world to myself, an eerie atmosphere enveloped the scene; glowering Quinag on the one hand and frowning Canisp (2779 feet) on the other, with the ruined castle of Ardvreck standing by the end of the loch all seemed to have me imprisoned in the great valley.

Another, twin-gabled, ruin gauntly stood, sinister in outlook, known as the White House officially, yet being Inverchalda House after the Chalda burn flowing close by. One could well imagine tormented spirits moaning and meandering in such a situation of loneliness, but my thoughts were interrupted by the purring of a car engine. Lights gradually neared me, until at last a voice hailed my name, the car still proceeding to a layby. A figure came running and then two more, slowly, yes, it was first Harry Owen and Dylis, and Mrs Campbell, who had all come to see if I was safe and sound near my journey's end. It was a fine thought that prompted their goodwill, and as we left each other the leaving lingered—until the throbbing engine's voice was silenced by the enfolding distance.

It was a good thing the Owens had earlier in the day brought me to locate my boarding-house accommodation, or I would have broken my neck in the darkness finding it. However seeing the lighted cottage, I stumbled along the dark path to where the Misses Corbett, the cat and the dog Papilons, all gave me a belated welcome to Inchnadamph.

5 *Facts and Fears*

One doesn't attempt a long journey of some duration without a few misgivings, but now after four days my confidence was assured. I had been afraid of the extra ten pounds to carry more than my intention, and now I knew I was able to accomplish my daily quota. What I did intend also was to obtain interesting folklore and history of places near to my route and Inchnadamph is such a place to make enquiries for such information. The guide-book will tell us that there is the largest waterfall in Britain hereabouts, four times the height of Niagara, and of the monument standing on a rising called the hill of Donaig—Cnoc-na-Donaig. This pillar is a gladdening reminder to all folk who love the north-west of the great work done by Peach and Home—two geologists who opened up this vast area to those interested in such pursuits, and whose written treatise is still considered a standard work for geological data.

However, the Misses Corbett, my hosts—Ruby the local school-mistress, and her sister Barbara, who transports children to and from school, attends to the school dinners, runs the house, feeds the hens and helps with visitors—were able to satisfy me with interesting facts about the area.

In the house—one-storied, under the shadow of a great rocky buttress—where I was staying, the Corbetts and their parents before them had lived. This house is neighboured by one 300 yards away and formerly one near to also, for the Scottish scene in the Highlands usually has three cottages close together for company. Such a condition here in between the high mountains sheltered on three sides and warm from the south-west sun had been particularly delectable for the one cottage on a hillock, and further sheltered by trees. It had a beautiful garden, especially for those parts, and its two elderly occupants felt their home to be a palace, occasionally being visited by their teacher daughter for her holidays.

One night the sublimity was shattered by screams of terror as the cottage became engulfed with fire, but before the inmates' neighbours could reach the cottage, it was too late—the poor folk had perished. The grief-stricken daughter, hearing of the terrible tragedy, returned to deal with the consequences, but could no longer return to such a place, fraught with such sad memories.

Some years later, yet another couple, seeing such a delightful spot, with its view, its arbour of trees, and its two neighbouring cottages, decided they too would like a home on the selfsame site. They cleared the ruin and eventually had a splendid cottage like as before standing there with its lovely garden. Wait! All went well for a long time, until fire broke out with such ferocity that the two occupants narrowly escaped with their lives. This was too much; the poor folk would not, could not, dare not, rebuild their little home again out of the tragic ruin, and left for ever.

The remains of this second conflagration were bulldozed to the ground, leaving a clear area amongst the trees and so it remained for a number of years, until a few years ago, when a motorist and his grown-up daughter came along, touring with a caravan behind their car, and there on the little knoll they decided to park for the night and did so.

All was calm amidst the marvellous mountains, away from maddening crowds, the occupants having fallen asleep when "FIRE", screamed the young woman; but as she opened the door, the inrush of air added to the extension of the flames and only with superhuman efforts did she drag her father from certain death. Nothing but twisted and blackened metal was left on the mound, the remains of a pyre sparked off to satisfy a demon of the Highlands? Coincidence? Redress?

The ruined castle and the White House earlier mentioned have a grim history. Ardvreck Castle, built on a small peninsula which juts into the Loch Assynt near Inchnadamph, was a stronghold of a Neil MacCleod and his wife Christina. It was here where MacCleod sheltered the Marquis of Montrose who had fled, after aiding King Charles II invading near Carbisdale, but without success. On hearing that the Government offered £25,000 for Montrose, MacCleod yielded to the temptation and allowed the fugitive into government hands; but withal the fortune did not last and having no issue and being held in contempt by most people, he and his wife gradually passed into oblivion.

In the meantime Ardvreck Castle and lands became possessed by a sect of the Mackenzies, who for some reason disliked the abode, and had the twin-gabled building made whose ruins I had passed in the twilight. The place is still named White House and has a brief but chilling history—it should be 'scorching' too. Inverchalda House properly named was built and lived in only a fortnight; for the imposing building housed a large party in celebration of its being occupied, the revelries continuing into a Sabbath morning when the house perished in flames.

I had been unaware the district was supposedly haunted—as I walked and finished at Inchnadamph in the darkness!

Three hundred years ago a seer in those parts named MacKenzie also prophesied that a rowan tree would grow from the roof of the house, where, upon its reaching a man's height, there would be a war in Assynt. There is such a tree whose stature is such, and long since, as the following suggests, this prognostication has had its apparent fulfilment, for an old intelligent lady who died only a year ago related this story, that in former times before the Corbetts lived in the house, a road mender and his four sons had occupation. They were poor and having no cow, one of the boys would fetch milk from the Lady's home at Achmore. One summer evening when the lad arrived he was plainly frightened; upon enquiries, they showed he had been sitting by the roadside in that area of peace and beauty when he saw a regiment of soldiers passing by. Then they mysteriously vanished into the sunset. Of course he was ridiculed, but yet a few years later, when the Great War broke out, his story undoubtedly stirred some men in the area to recruit. A few of the demobilized soldiers—now old—rose to eminence in Glasgow Police Force and elsewhere.

I was invited to see the school functioning next day, and rising early in my little outshot room, I drew the curtains and there under the gigantic escarpment, released from various huts, were fowls pecking and strutting about—not penned up in some vile prisons called battery systems. Miss Barbara with the cat about her shoulders like a living fur, strolled around the croft talking to one and another of her livestock, as she released birds from their pens, and then quite evidently returned to make my breakfast.

I returned the half-mile back to the school to take a photograph of a highland junior department in session, and though I have in my experience seen many school rooms, with as many differing disciplines, this room with its seventeen boys and girls with Miss Ruby Corbett as their teacher constituted one of the happiest I have ever seen. After my introduction I was asked to scrutinize their work, which revealed a state of real efficiency, and then proceeded to take a photograph.

I had passed the old school with its small translucent windows, where children behind them could never have seen the sky or trees or waving grass, and passed further—nearer the Loch Assynt—to the new airy wood and glass structure, a delight to learn in, the building not yet a year old.

I determined to be in Elphin before dark and set out the ten miles down the long valley between east and west mountains of 2400 to 2800 feet altitudes. The roads formerly unfenced, except in the villages, were now bordered by wire fences keeping livestock and sheep in their various stockades. As I neared a large farm with a magnificent lawn, which would have done justice to a Cambridge college, the lady invited me into the spacious kitchen for a snack. It was from this fine home that her child went to the school I had recently left and from the windows of which Miss Barbara's vehicle would be seen coming to collect her passenger along with those from Elphin.

The road once humpy over the undulating terrain had not long been evened out, straightened, and made double width to avoid the use of passing places. It was on here, occasionally, a tourist car would pass at a leisurely speed, its occupants enjoying the beauty of the landscape. I was to experience almost certain death on such a road on two occasions, had I not jumped into the ditch or mud to avoid two maniacs—dashing 'full out' to the top of Scotland, one day, and to

Gretna the next, when of course they would have 'seen Scotland'.

This warm sunny afternoon gently sprang a surprise on me, for far away like two dots were two walkers. As we approached I noted their weariness and resolved to cheer them up with a chocolate bar between us. The man handsome and young, like so many more had 'a string attached' and walked alongside a beautiful female, nude—but for her shoes. She had no cares and eyed me gently with soft eyes with long lashes. Her neck, so graceful, was covered by long dark hair, in fact she was gorgeous. I spoke to both in turn, the man first, as I didn't wish to arouse jealousy and to avoid its possibility, I broke off three pieces of chocolate, giving him the first piece and her the second. That was my undoing, for her eyes asked for more. She was so beautiful I wanted to put my arm about her neck, but before taking this advantage asked if I could photograph them both. It was agreed, but not before more chocolate was distributed and well before I had consumed mine a warm nose thrust against my hand for more, you'll guess, of course, she was a horse (or more correctly a mare).

The young man, fond of his animals, replied to my questioning about shoeing them in these remote areas and said that a farrier would come out quarterly from Inverness with a workshop van carrying ready-made shoes which, if needing some modification for individual animals, could be heated by cylinder gas fire, and re-shaped on a small anvil.

We reluctantly parted, again becoming like small specks on that huge landscape, my only company being sheep in the largest flocks I saw on the whole journey, and if for any reason sleep ever avoids me, there will my mind wander with more than enough sheep to count 'to send me off'.

Trailing on, a junction gave two alternatives, Inverness by Bonar Bridge or towards Ullapool. I took the planned one and photographed my haversack and a tremendous length of telephone wires supported by their poles which like a long line of troops went on and on into the vast oblivion. Poles and wires are usually the bane of photographers, but on this late afternoon the lines glistened like silver harp-strings in the fierce sunlight, and but for the help of a halted motorist I couldn't have taken the shot for glare. I gave him directions and he held a cushion for its shadow to shield the lens—it worked!

It was an afternoon of lonesomeness—easy going, no physical strain, and but for the horseman and the motorist and his wife in the open, four hours went by without me having a word with anyone. Here it was that I had to train myself into taking keener observation of natural life about me, for I was missing human company. Having hoisted my pack for the last time, the last three miles soon were covered, with my eyes squinting from the fierce sparkling of sun and water, and again I was enthralled by the sight of a magnificent panorama of mountains, as I rounded the shoulder of Canisp's range. It seemed to be none other than a Norwegian scene, with sharp-edged contours thrusting into the cloudless heavens with Cam Loch, brilliant as quicksilver, before me.

Only a Turner could have endeavoured to capture those deep blues and greys of near and more distant mountains with their aura of yellow, turquoise, pink and purple skies about them. It was an unforgettable sight, made more wonderful than ever, when, as approaching the little sporadic broken line of dwellings I asked for my host's address, the ladies chatting at the lattice gate said: "We knew you were coming, the children have told us so."

6 *Getting Into my Stride*

AFTER a night on an improvised bed in the full Suilven guest house I was ready to leave the fine hospitality of Ina Macdonald and her ageing sisters Jemima and Barbara. Two young Berkshire guests from the dormer windowed bedroom called and insisted on a car run for me to see Stack Polly—the mountain climbers' practising ground. The scene is immense, being swallowed in hazy distance, the approach being along the still old one-track road, by an eerie lochan. I was glad of the break before my seventeen miles' greatest stint, and was glad to be shown what hill climb would have to be encountered soon.

Gerald and Gillian Harding, and Ina and her sisters, were soon waving me off from Elphin's little line of houses, modernized and painted in bright colours, each competing with the others for beautiful appearance. The old school, roofless, looked sad in comparison by the old road, while parentally, the grand mountains over 2000 feet soared around in Norwegian splendour, indeed the names Suilven and Canisp suggest such an origin.

I passed the phone kiosk which for once didn't function, whereas all others through polite operators got me through to home every night, some giving me a pleasant word as they heard 'Dronfield': "Och, yes, I know, near Sheffield." Then came the last houses before a tremendous journey via Knockan, with a little church for the smallest of hamlets. Its few cottages stood up off the new road, railed off for protection of children playing. An old 'retired' spinning wheel stood by one door, where I was invited in to see the old lady who had used it formerly to spin the soft wool of the Cheviot breed of sheep. Old Mrs Henrietta Macleod, now eighty-six and retired from her spinning, lives with her daughter in an immaculate cottage, where the old lady spoke of changing times from horse-drawn vehicles to motor vans which provide fresh and varied foods and better pharmaceutical services, making life much more pleasant. Gone are the days of digging peat now coal is brought to the door, gone collecting water from the well or drying brook. Now the stream waters are conserved high up the mountains, and filtered and piped to the houses.

The bright enamelled gas stove and fireplace and electric light shade indicated the fast modernization taking place in faraway hamlets; and now with a double width road they were seeing more tourists visiting the far north.

Their walls were beautifully decorated and festooned with two indications of fealty, one to the Lord and the other to the Queen. Large religious pictures occupied walls, and china scriptural ornaments the mantel-shelf. Large portraits of royalty or regal festival occasions were on view showing the evident patriotism of the Scottish people. One man expressed his view saying, "We should sing to the British Queen with the British National Anthem."

The 'brew' over, "Goodbye", we said, and leaving the valley I steadily attacked the 600-feet rise between the mountains, passing in the distance five hinds and a stag beyond the deer fence. Then a large ranch carrying a fine herd of cattle showed what good use can be applied to the vast acreage of some mountain country once left desolate.

It was up here in the silence where a head-splitting roar from a jet which passed immediately overhead to clear the pass made my head ache for half an hour—obviously I had reached civilization.

Downhill now, unsheltered from blazing heat, made me glad to see a stream with a few alders. Here I dined, and bathed my feet, as yet wearing well, using two pairs of socks for cushioning.

Two downcast hikers impatiently waiting for a 'thumb lift' thought I was mad as I set off again for distant Ullapool, passing between pine trees by a reedy lochan—a superb framing for the distant Stack Polly. Anyone in the vicinity of Ullapool should see this magnificence, for it is like a Canadian or New Zealand landscape in the wilds of unspoilt natural beauty.

It is hereabouts where tourists, having reached thus far north, seem to turn about, missing the wild freedom and grandeur of Sutherland, for here began the pattern of the changing scene, as when, arriving at the hamlet of Kanaird where I delivered a letter from Elphin, I saw busy haymakers —with the children home from school and the sheepdogs, either riding on the tractor drays or wildly rolling and tossing in the scented hay.

Leaving them, another fierce but short steep forced the sweat from every pore, and I could not assuage my raging thirst, for some streams near roads have either a dead sheep rotting nearby or carelessly dispensed rubbish and are somewhat risky to drink from, unless the water is obtained from upstream—but this is not always available, being fenced. Seeing a car approaching steadily I held my flask downwards indicating no liquid suggesting I needed a drink. The car halted and a tartan-skirted lady said, "No water, sir, orange."

"No thanks, just water will do."

"Have orange, sir," she repeated, as the young handsome man opened a tin and filled my flask.

"How much do I owe you for this kindness, please?"

"Nothing, sir; the pleasure is ours."

"I am indeed grateful to you. What is your address? I will one day send you a photograph to remind you of your nice gesture to a stranger."

I knew she was Scottish because of the tartan; then she informed me, in perfect English, "Our address is Frau Helma and Herr Keiko Bels, Bremerhaven, Germany."

I should have known this mother and son were not of Scottish nationality since such ladies leave the wearing of tartans to their husbands who wear kilts.

My newly-found friends left southwards, leaving me to enjoy the drink in peace, then more leisurely to follow, reaching the Strath at Ardmair as the sun slipped silently from an ocean of blue into a sea of gold, turning to crimson as it touched that mysterious dividing line between the heavens and earth.

Only another three miles and a 200-foot climb to cover, as the changing colours of the terrain changed to deep sombre browns under a pink afterglow with the sea loch's waters a silvery sheen, and when at the top of the gentle rise I looked ahead, the twinkling lights of Ullapool's fishing port welcomed me as to an Arabian palace, there the first folk to greet me on the first corner were my new friends the Bels, who said, "Hello—we meet again." As I ambled on the foreshore I felt amazingly fit after seventeen miles' glorious walking, but felt jolly glad to see Mrs Lawton, the youth hostel warden who had reserved me accommodation and said, "Mr Kyme, what on earth will you be doing next?" I could have said, "Eating and sleeping!"

7 *Taking a Short Cut*

I FARED excellently in the Ullapool youth hostel as usual and found my companions at the breakfast table to be foreign visitors. This superb village by Loch Broom with its fishing trade, long, low cottages and modern boarding establishments seems to be the northern Mecca of most travellers, and from its shops and stores they can get anything from a 'rig out' to a case of cutlery.

Mrs Lawton saw me off with "God speed", and amidst the conglomeration of fishing boats, yachts, and squealing gulls I found the ferry—not for the summer isles, but simply to cross to Aultnaharrie. By this less than a mile crossing, my journey was shortened by eighteen miles, and, had I kept to the road, my day's journey would have situated me out in the wilds choose what the weather. My goal was to be Badcaul by Little Loch Broom.

Before the ferry boat loaded the little assembly of passengers gathered on the pier steps, while a motley group surveyed us curiously. One, a very flashy lady bedecked with a flamboyant show of jewellery, eyed me from head to foot and asked, "Are you on tour, sir?"

"Yes madam."

"Where to sir, a long distance?"

"Fairly, madam."

"Do tell me please, where?"

"Dover, madam."

"*Walking*?"

"Yes, madam, but for the ferries."

"Oh, I *wish* I could come with you," she said as she grasped me by both hands, her fair, fifties face beaming into mine, while her silent, solemn husband looked on—probably thinking: I wish he would take her for good!

My cap and stockings were red and my face the same colour,

as she continued her questioning chatter, but thankfully the ferry loaded, and 'plopped' its way round the jetty and set off obliquely towards the other side. Privileged to use the tiller and soon across, I started off from the few old stone houses at Aultnaharrie, being accompanied by some pleasant people up the very steep track to the saddle between Bein Ghobhlach and Blarnalevoch.

As we looked back across the loch we were thrilled by the sight of Ullapool and sat to have a meal, little knowing that on the saddle, some gruesome interments had long since taken place on the broad area out of sight of the water. My evening's host said how the old fishing folk in times of strong superstition feared that people who died of certain complaints, if buried in locations overlooking the sea, would spoil herring catches and so the wild tops away from the lochs and the village became this weird cemetery.

My companions returned ferrywards as I struck out on the other side, whistling the 'Mingulay Boat Song', as the 600-feet altitude steadily diminished down the side of the afforested mountain, looking across towards An Teallach (3483 feet) and companion heights beyond Dundonnell. The scenery was glorious. I once walked the one-track road and saw no one for three miles and now I met a joiner, a postman wearing green spectacles driving his van to the peninsula hamlet of Badrallach, then the nurse and midwife, and finally a council workman with a large lorry.

Nurse Evelyn Butler from Hampshire told me she and her invalid husband manage a croft with various stock, and sell milk to the local tea-shop. Before a complement of two Jersey cows was satisfactorily reached, they had one beast—Morag—which had to leave the holding. Bought believed in calf, facts proved in deficiency, for soon after being in custody at the croft Morag showed a determined restlessness in her nature. She would break out instinctively in the direction where she thought she would 'get her way'. Nurse Butler, questioned by an old lady about the farm and its progress, was told "Her trouble is, she is wanting her way with a gentleman." The pure-bred Jersey bull was too far away for availability, so the old lady suggested that three fences and the burn would prevent Morag's escape. But the cow of an adamant nature cleared any and every obstacle to keep her in the croft, needing many hands to get her back if only temporarily, so she was sold regretfully, as the nurse so wanted pure-bred calves for her stock.

As for the lorry driver, when the nurse, reversing her car for him to squeeze past at the road junction, asked, "Do you know how far this fellow is walking?", he gasped and grasped my hand like a vice so that I almost needed Nurse Butler's professional help. This nurse-midwife needs courage besides her medical skill, since she has to go out on dark nights on lonely roads in all weathers and cross the loch by boat, besides having to walk long distances to attend to her patients; later I was to hear how much she is respected by all around for so much depends on her skill and devotion to duty to the community.

We parted, and taking her advice I passed the huge pines, beeches and other deciduous trees in the warm humid valley, taking the route of Mrs Dumphie's footbridge suspended over the shallow river, due to dry weather. Passing through fields, two sheepdogs approached followed by a boy, and fearing the dogs, I shouted: "Will they bite?" "Och, no," so we joined forces and went into a gloomy barn. Again I called out, "Anyone alive in here?" "Och, aye" came the reply, when, as my sight became inured to the conditions, I saw two farmers, a youth, four children and two more dogs all lolling about on sacks and hay bales, finding it too hot to work or play outside. We had a long chat, some conjuring and eventually a photograph, surprisingly not including the personage of Rip Van Winkle, who I'm sure must have been somewhere in the barn.

The large company returned to hibernation as I went on through Ardessie with its typical Scottish cottage and adjacent rowan tree. I had passed Ardessie a number of times before—but in a car—and missed a fine sight; but walking I immediately saw a two leap waterfall, above the bridge, with a young tree growing from a rocky fissure between the leaps.

The country hereabouts with its mountains and Little Loch Broom, is breath-taking, confined to the simple shapes of shoreland, hill, and mountain, a restful change to the eye as opposed to the many-angled outlines of the big city.

The peninsula with Badrallach lay like a Loch Ness

Monster snoozing in the shimmering waters, and as a change from lying down for ten minutes—as in an afternoon I would —I went on towards a little house shop to treat myself to an ice-cream, etc.

To avoid a long trek round, I slid down a grassy slope, through a gateway, across a footbridge over a little stream which meanders low between rhododendron bushes, by an open path, between small tables and chairs, on to a paved area and finally to the door of the house shop.

Having nodded to three Americans, I knocked on the door and was approached by a small septuagenarian, short-cropped, white-haired lady, who curtly answered my salutation. Her knife-edged parting directed attention to two piercing eyes which overlooked thin steel-rimmed spectacles settled low on her sharp nose. Her gaze penetrated me as did the looks of Miss MacKenzie's tall sister and brother standing there in the background of the living apartment.

In the shop was the most excellent and precisely arranged show of commodities I have ever seen, for I learned the older sister and brother saw to that side of the business. There was everything, and somewhere a 'fridge', for I got my ice-cream and other oddments, making them last until the Americans went. Their departure led me to enquire politely if I might have the privilege of using a certain apartment. "Och aye, the place is way through the bushes." The journey was as lengthy as the approach to the shop, including a detour. I'm glad it wasn't dark in case a tiger had pounced from the bushes. However, ultimately a 'commodious' building was reached, fastened to supporting planks, almost cubical in shape, the door opening outwards. I entered, just being able to stand erect, and in the gloomy interior a long, low white wood bench scrupulously clean occupied the full length of one side. In the middle, a round aperture was evident, known in my young day as a 'one holer'. This apartment did not require a two holer as in the days of larger families, when sittings sometimes in urgency became coincidental. To provide the appearance of comfortable seating for this establishment, an oval frame of beautiful polished mahogany was reared against the back wall, brass-hinged for convenience in use. As a preliminary, a scrutiny was made for the chain pull, since there was no lever, and finding none, I wondered what form of flushing system there could be. Then I looked through and down the hole—Horrors! Down—way down—a long way down, was the little stream before mentioned which gently flows into the nearby Little Loch Broom.

No! I fled, for when I looked through and down, a blast of cold air poured from the shapely orifice, and therefore I considered it wiser to go out into the world and face the wind like a man, rather than be like some foolish folk who would sit there and suffer the chill winds of inexperience and indolence both in force and direction.

Up the slope I plodded to the road to Badcaul there to 'caul' it a day, and doing so Mrs Murdo Mackenzie with a fine twinkle in her eyes invited me into the finest of homely facilities provided by the Highlanders.

8 *Murdo, the Ross-shire Raconteur*

In seven days, I had as many different homes for apartments, all excellent in one way or another. This of Murdo Mackenzie and his wife was one in which I immediately felt at home, probably because we were in the same age range and had some similar interests. Their house and outbuilding were so nicely situated elevated from the old road; and furthermore, adjacent was their low shed which served as the local post office, making them familiar with all local happenings in the community. Also, such associations as they have with all the people who live scattered for miles around, provide them with the historical background of many of the crofters. However, even in contemporary history, people from other parts of the country move into a locality and take up occupations, so also in bygone days the same applied to the area of Dundonnell and district.

The above conditions were relevant to two of the accounts about which Murdo expounded; they are as follows. In the area around Dundonnell, many years ago, lived a very domineering headmistress of a school. She was imperious, and of course disliked by children, staff and local inhabitants. She had a husband; and not one servant, but three, this latter fact to prove to all around the importance of her status in the community. All the painstaking work of chores about her house done under duress was accounted as unworthy of her home, and such commands as "Repeat your work again girl, and put some effort into it. What will people think if I allow such slipshod work to go by without remonstration?" Of course visitors to the house saw the immaculate condition of everything in the home, but done in such servile circumstances.

Eventually, one of the servants would 'put up with it' no longer, and tendered a week's notice to terminate her service. A diatribe ensued. "Girl, what stupid notion has entered your head to desire to leave such a superior place of domestic service; you won't find anywhere else in these parts where you will fare so well. No, not in all Ross-shire! Well, if you are so adamant as to wish to leave, I suppose you must go."

The headmistress could not without difficulty get anyone to work for her, only those folk who would have to go far away from home, or could not get any other occupation. Thereupon the woman began to devise a plan to retain the girl at all costs—a wicked means.

At last, a miserable week went by, the servant being in the kitchen commiserating with and bidding goodbye to the other two, when in stormed the tyrant. "Someone has stolen five pounds." Three faces went red with the suddenness of the accusation. "Who is it?" demanded the woman. "Come along, *who* is it?" Of course none of them, and none answered. "Well then, I must discover for myself." She questioned each in turn and none would admit, of course. Then, the awful moment: "Girl, before you go, open your bag, to prove you are an innocent person!" The lass hesitated, she did not like the ignominy of having to do this in spite of her innocence. "Hurry girl, by your actions it would appear you are guilty; before you go, I will see myself one thing or the other. Out of the way!" The woman removed the few other belongings left in the bag the girl was slow to extricate, when "Ha, here it is, I thought as much, you wicked girl: you have disgraced your service here by this mean deed; further, your parents' good name has been ruined!"

The girl burst into tears. How was she to prove to the other servants her innocence? "Now girl, it is no use crying, you should have thought of the consequences before your action! Sobs!! There is only one way out open to you. I will say no more of this wickedness, if you will stay on and serve me. No one shall know of this." The girl thought, if she stayed on it would appear to the others that she was guilty, so she said she would leave. "All right girl, I shall take the matter to court if you insist on leaving: people must know of your dishonesty, folk like you are not worthy of being in service."

The lass went by the lonely road towards home, her mind torn with the problem of proving her innocence against a wily woman's plan. She occasionally sat by the roadside weeping, when at last a gig came by which halted and a gentleman descended to ask the cause of her tears. He reassured her of his good character by names he mentioned, of her parents and other folk known to her, and thus she took the opportunity to be driven home. While so doing, he told her he was on vacation from his work as a solicitor, and would be glad to take up her case against the headmistress. He knew what she was like and similarly he felt assured of the girl's innocence. He stipulated that, when having thought of the procedure he would inform her what to say to the court.

The court day came and the room was agog with its full complement of folk eager to know the truth. "Can it be that this nice girl we respect has stooped to thieving, or is this woman we hate accusing her wrongly? We'll see."

Madam testified on questioning how she had to, reluctantly against her will, resort to emptying the remnants of the girl's bag, since the wench was so furtive in doing so. "And, there it was in her clothing!"

"Thank you, madam! Now girl, stand and testify as to why you say you are innocent when the money was found in your possession."

All ears strained, the girl looking at the solicitor for reassurance; then at the Magistrate. "Your worship, I myself and the other two girls I worked with, and madam's husband knew that she would be away in school certain times of the day, so then and while the girls were busy in another part of the house, the teacher's husband said he would put five pounds in my bag if I would go to bed with him."

Hardly had she spoken this when the headmistress shouted "She is a liar, I put it there myself!"

The other story Murdo Mackenzie told me I will relate as we reach Gruinard Bay in our 'walk' together. Murdo is six years older than myself, wiry, weather-beaten, grey, bent, and great pals with his rough-haired sheepdog, this latter getting on in years—'age for age'—as old as his master. We

Above: Some of my first footprints in a million and more strides, beginning on the north-west coast beyond this wild, windswept Balnakeil Bay. *Below:* Sequel to wind and weather – a ruined cottage at Durness

‘Will you please photograph my two salmon?’

Loch Glencoul at Unapool

The sun dips low on Loch Assynt

The school in session at Inchnadamph

Elphin with its new houses and the old, ruined school

This delayed-action photograph shows the author (*left*) walking with Murdo MacKenzie, the raconteur of Badcaul, and his dog

The artist John Fielder

The living-room of a crofter's cottage near Gairloch

Scotch drizzle on Loch Maree

A Highland cow

Unavailingly, I waited ages for someone to walk along the road into one of Scotland's loveliest villages – Shieldaig

A lobster boat off the Kyle of Loch Alsh; the Cuillins are in the background

all enjoyed the hour-by-hour tales he told us that night I called in. How often he had told the others before I don't know, but they listened with eagerness, occasionally butting in with some question or fact. There was Annie, his wife, who cooked me a herring meal (I shall always remember, I was so hungry), then their daughter-in-law who is the post mistress, and finally a taller young fellow, wiry, reddish-faced, smart, wearing dark sun-glasses—I'd seen him before somewhere his son, the postman, who goes in his van all round for miles. The narration had to cease—bed!

After breakfast, before my departure, we mutually agreed that a photograph of Murdo, his dog, and myself together, walking on the 'old road' alongside the 'new' one actually in process of making, would be an idea—to show progress in those northern parts of Scotland. It proved rather comical, I was adamant that all photos for the book would be taken by myself (no, not conceit), therefore the delayed action system would have to be set in operation. No tripod: I didn't want to carry one and a half pounds extra weight for 800 miles, so we devised an arrangement of kitchen steps and a clamp for the camera support. Only ten seconds for me to run to position alongside Murdo and his dog, from setting the shutter in motion, was a difficult feat. We were all involved and rehearsed twice, yet when Mrs Mackenzie Jnr shouted "fire" we assumed Murdo, the dog and myself would be walking, away to the distant Highlands. Not so; it turned out to be like a changing of the baton in a relay sports event. Murdo, not used to acrobatics, became confused and appeared to be reluctant to give me my stick, hence the 'tug of war'. I hope my publisher will have the photograph as an illustration; it is not a masterpiece, but I feel sure it will cause amusement to the folk at Badcaul.

Like at other places, I had been so happy with them it was a mental tug of war to leave. Annie Mackenzie I knew would have prepared nice 'eats' for me and a coffee flask filled—including the pinch of salt for energy and tang. She had, and I was off, burdened with a heavy load—yes, of happy memories.

Every now and again as I turned to look back on 'Rosemount', Badcaul, there were waving hands, even until figures and houses merged into the greyness of distance integral to the Highlands.

9 *Striding High*

SOON Badcaul, the epitome of the Highland landscape, was gone, the road-makers keeping busy as I passed and soon the long, lonely road was to myself. Beyond, to the far south-west as I descended the moorland road, could be seen the Cuillins on Skye—only in Switzerland had I ever seen the equal for a clarity of fifty miles. Down I swept past the suckling lambs and fighting sheep, all occupying the road, until reaching the large farm, with enclosed fields open to the afternoon sun, where I looked in at the yawning doorway. No one stirred in this stone-built house with its broad, open stairway and plaited red cord handrail with shining ferrules; perhaps 'they' had gone for a swim in Gruinard Bay, just beyond the large trees in the sheltered steep valley.

Gruinard Bay is singularly beautiful, having the impact of Symond's Yat, or Beachy Head; yet today a large War Department notice-board 'disallows' anyone to approach the Island because of anthrax danger. Supposedly in the event of enemy invasion in the last war, cattle were to have been infected with germs from this dreadful scourge and released amongst other cattle roaming in the Highlands, which would eventually have made the land uninhabitable. Gruinard Island, being used as a 'base' for this probable operation, is now out-of-bounds to everyone for many years to come.

The bay, sheltered by high ground and with a gently sloping beach, is ideal for bathers, and leaving 'all my worldly goods' with a bank manager I was in the briny in no time. It was exquisite on this hot day to laze about in the clear water and watch the effect of light on the rippled sand beneath the gentle waves. Never in my life had I felt fitter and as the swim finished, the 'banker' was safe, and his wife and daughter had prepared a delicious meal for the four of us—I never obtained their address!

The bay seemed soon to be deserted, the cars chugging out of the deep hollow southwards. As for myself, the cooling swim made the going much easier. To pass the top round the rock shoulder at any time without looking back would be a sin, so I took this as an excuse to stand and stare, then moved on the high plateaux fast towards Aultbea.

Plodding on at Laide, a door was open at a cottage where I was obliged for a drink, when the man asked, "Mister, where are you going this time o'day, Aultbea?"

"Yes, sir."

"What and walking?"

"Yes, sir."

"You'd——carry me," his remark being probably in unprintable Gaelic.

It was Saturday evening and going dusk after my strenuous day in the sun, when after a stretch in the open, the 'egg shell' seascape was broken by a darkening mass of land jagged sharply by cottage rooftops and chimneys. There was a yellow glow, square in the black side of a timber dwelling, which proved to be a shop where, when I knocked and entered, the takings were being counted for the day. The shop-keeper stocked up my iron rations, and then for the last stint, I plodded on past a few crofts, some with stone walls like castle battlements, when out of the silence a shattering *roar* made me tremble. The wall spoke! Again, and again, and when level with its 'mouthpiece', I saw silhouetted the black muzzle, head and horns of a bull thrust over the wall, bellowing across the road to where dimly some black shapes of disinterested cows were feeding in another field.

It soon was dark, when I recalled Old Murdo's tale of these old crofts around Gruinard area, when he was young. Sheep used the island for summer pasturage, being taken to and removed from it by boat loads, shepherds, dogs, and 'factor'-manager carrying out the operations. He told me how when sheep were returning home to the laird's home grounds one day, a crofter's dog so savaged a worker dog that a terrible mêlée ensued with dogs, sheep and shepherds. The factor, a notoriously brutal man, addressed the crofter—whose dog was only protecting his property. "He'll none do that again." "What do you mean?" "You'll see."

The factor then wrote out six notices to farmers to quit their crofts, thus losing their homes and livelihoods; they were soon dispersed, causing a great tragedy. On hearing of the factor's ruthless show of authority, the laird was deeply distressed, but could do nothing when the damage had been done, so he offered the working crofts to a good farmer to keep in order. This man refused, indicating it was against his principle to reap benefits from the industry of people who had been wrongfully evicted, so the crofts went to ruin and the land back to rough heath.

It was fortunate that I knew Aultbea in the light, and looked for the twinkling lights of the naval docks; but before shouldering the last rise, a passing couple in their car offered me a lift, being astonished at my polite refusal, and then gradually drew away into the inky gloom of night-time, myself glad to follow the merging red glow of tail lights.

Eventually the sporadic display of single lights showed Aultbea with village and dock illumination. Sources of enquiry suggested directions to the youth hostel, which, if I had seemingly followed them, I would have soon been given a watery grave. (I shuddered next morning on seeing where I had been heading.) After quite half an hour, being only a few minutes away from my venue, I saw a chink of light which afforded me fresh 'illumination', for when having grovelled for booby traps of steps, palings and barbed wire, I found a door, which on being knocked, a timid voice in Scottish enquired from the bathroom "What do you want?" "A guardian angel," would have been a suitable answer. However getting down to bare facts, it was the solution to my problem; the 'voice' guided me aright.

How on earth my clothes were not in shreds is a mystery, and on opening the door to the hostel, pairs of eyes from young and old stared on me from top to bottom, some folk asking where I had come from. On being informed, one kindly soul pressed the bell push to save me the minimum of effort to acquaint Han, the warden, of my belated appearance, who to her lasting credit made an excellent meal for me when I should have cooked my own.

10 *A Day to Remember*

Before I was off on my second Sunday morning, Han with an air of officialdom gave me a personal chore, involving the shaking of four carpets and replacing same. Seeing a juvenile hosteller I asked if he would care to assist me, and next thing I was being chased round the room by Warden with a poker—"Do the chore yourself, you idle good-for-nothing!" she demanded with a wicked twinkle in her eye, the boy being relieved on realizing we were racing about in fun. All hostel wardens are original people for some special trait in their characters, having special abilities, probably in botany, art, photography, athletics, languages, or for spontaneous good humour like Han. I asked her for a local 'twist' of humour and this story of Aultbea follows.

There is near Loch Ewe, out from the village, an island, and when a middle-aged bachelor touring the locality asked a young lady "Where does this road lead, please?"

"To Gruinard, sir," she said.

"Whose are those big boats?"

"Oh they are naval vessels, sir."

"What is the name of the island, miss, please?"

Her answer became very indistinct as she shyly replied.

"I'm sorry miss, will you repeat the answer, I didn't quite hear you?"

"Isle of Ewe, sir."

"Yes my dear, I love you too," he said, sweeping her off her feet, and soon the wedding bells rang.

I was off, disregarding advice from an ageing woman who told me the night before, not to walk on the Lord's day. She had kindly directed me to the hostel and advised me to remain there until Monday: "You rest on the Sabbath, the rest will do you good."

I had before breakfast looked at the anchorage where I saw no one and no one stirred in the straggly village on walking through: only cooing doves in the sycamores by the church heralded that glorious morning. I would have worshipped with the congregation but could not afford to leave later, as I was compelled to be in Gairloch before dark to obtain apartments.

I left the last cottages and the hotel and climbed into the steep road and looking back, the village looked like a sailing ship with her sails limp in an ocean becalmed as no sign of life was visible until I was high above the loch, when a distant purr heralded an outboard motor-boat weaving a widening trail in the dappled waters.

I had well passed the neatest camouflaged War Department installations I have ever seen, for the huge oil storage tanks are only noticeable to folk who are aware of their presence, and soon was rounding the wild heathlands towards Inverewe.

Up there between Aultbea and Inverewe there is a layby at a viewpoint where the magnificence of Torridon and mountains round Loch Maree can be seen. On a good day at least thirty-six peaks can be counted. It is Gruinard with a difference, the one is of sea and islands, and the other a view of mountains, wonderful at anytime, but ecstatic in winter when snowcapped.

Down I went, a swing in my stride, towards Tuirnaig overpowered by a strong scent of silage issuing from a large farm; but undeterred pressed on to one of the finest spots in 800 miles. To look along the small loch across to the mountains is breathtaking, particularly so when the sun shines from a forward position, giving added sparkle to the water and sharpness and contrast to the mountains. The primeval landscape in this area is Scotland epitomized; and not to be outdone, a stone's throw away is the world famous garden of Inverewe, which has been developed over the last century by bringing shiploads of good soil for a suitable growing medium for many varieties of plants, shrubs and trees, many of which are exotic.

Coachloads of people milling about were as numerous as at Hyde Park Gate on a Sunday. Some spoke to me who were Belgians, and yet again I met my friends the Johnsons in this paradise of horticulture, warmed by the Gulf stream and where frost is unknown.

The scheme's originator, a Mr Osgood Mackenzie of Inverewe, who also wrote *A Hundred Years in the Highlands,* bequeathed the project to his daughter who on becoming Mrs Sawyer gave proceeds of takings to support the District Nursing Association. Later, before her death, she ensured the property and proceeds would become a responsibility of the National Trust.

Elbowing out of the busy gardens and passing the sea loch, Poolewe was reached in the mid-afternoon, but sound asleep. No one was about, and yet parched to the limit on this hot day, I searched for water. A door to a cottage was open; I knocked, and soon a tall, gentle, white-haired, pale blue eyed lady asked me in. All I wanted was a drink and for my flask to be filled. Ushered into the immaculate front room, where I scarce dare enter because of my rough boots, she asked me to sit in an easy chair. The 'water' was a long time coming and while waiting, an inventory of this palace showed a clavicord, an elephant carved from teak with ivory tusks, toes and eyes—the finest I've ever seen—and a mahogany table so finely polished I first placed my cap on it before laying my camera thereon.

My inventory ceased as Mrs Rose came in bearing a beautiful tray covered with a lovely array of food and coffee; and having finished my tea, she filled my flask.

"How much do I owe you please for all your kindness?"

"The pleasure is mine," or words to that effect.

I was moved by this act of goodwill, more so when I learned later how the Sabbath must not be made a day of work, or to be a day of unnecessary moving from place to place. Mrs Rose believes that every day should be a Sabbath to honour God's name, and do His will by helping anyone who is in need. The information she gave me about Poolewe in the old days is that people eked out a living by working small crofts, and rearing a stirk—a year-old calf—and selling this to pay the rent. They also fished for herrings and white fish and some also had hill pasture for sheep and cattle.

At annual sales of older cattle and stirks, a large family would buy a cow for milking, whereas two smaller families would purchase one between them; later in winter the beast would be slaughtered for meat. Salt, the preservative for the carcass, was also used for the catches of fish not consumed immediately. Some farmers also kept pigs, but on my travels I saw few in Scotland.

She said how the superstitions were dying, such as regarding the rowan tree by the cottage, replacing which has sprung up a deeply religious faith. Local folk do no work on a Sunday which can be done any other day, but those said to be 'broader minded' treated Sunday as every other day and frequently disregarded God anyway.

Male labour today is concerned with road-making and maintenance, house-building and related trades, and now to the delight of all, some are employed with the electricity schemes which keep houses heated and lighted and provide energy for so many facilities never before available to these remote villages.

Some men, I found later, would not for all the wealth in the world move from their own localities, and the NATO base at Aultbea had been a source of employment to some who did not want to leave for the cities.

A great day out for folk is to be off to Inverness at 7.30 a.m. by coach, to have a meal, go shopping, another meal, and return about 8.30—a long day, and for 30*s*. fare, a grand run.

It was impossible to remember all she told me, but Mrs Rose so kindly fulfilled her promise and sent a fine informative letter, as so many others have done to provide me with local lore and knowledge.

"Anything unusual, do you recall, Mrs Rose?"

"Yes, once, though we don't often get snow, we had a very hard winter with much of it, which lingered long, and to our astonishment was pink at any time of day—not with sunrises or sunsets. We did reckon that it was due to falling ash from much wood burning which caused the beautiful colouring."

I left this lovely Christian home gleaming brightly, seeing the stone steps leading to her back garden, and turned out at the front door—but there was no one about. We said "Goodbye," and off through the tree-lined road, by the river, up to the moorland, I passed the end of the magnificent Loch Maree, where on a dark night one can see all of twenty miles along the full length—and up Glen Docherty—the trail of car lights as they come down the pass. Here yet again one must pause to see this great sight of loch and mountain, it is awe-inspiring indeed—oh! but do put on some midge repellent, smear some soap on every vulnerable part, or wait until mid-September and they may be gone.

Between Aultbea and Gairloch youth hostel (Carn Dearg) this last rise of moor to Loch Tollie is hard going; but it is worth every ounce of energy to see this sheet of water against the light with its brooding dark mass of mountain and blue sky, and a parchment white surface, it is fantastic—a Turner masterpiece. I went on between the rocks—raced on for Gairloch to get some apartments—when I heard, "Hello Hector, how are you?" a voice said through a car window, "Like some tea? Let's sit down while we have it." It was my great friend Bob Crawford—and his wife—a youth hostel official at head offices, who had been told by Mrs Lawton approximately where they would find me. I was overjoyed.

It seemed strange I couldn't accept a lift; they left, and soon disappeared along the road. overshadowed by dark pines, and myself following to a rhythmic sound of boots all alone on a perfect, fast-fading Sunday evening.

I had missed church services this day and strangely thought of home; but found the fulfilment of an aboriginal craving to be alone with God in the wilds, pitting myself against the elements and striving unaided by mechanical means of travel. I had seen magnificence unparalleled all week, and met people with true nobility of character, whose chief aim in life was to give unstinted service to other folk. This journeying, in spite of sweat and blisters, of burning thirst, of new beds, and mixed diets, had passed my wildest dreams—oh yes, the thirty-pound pack, I'd forgotten it. Besides, the Johnsons were taking home for me a few ounces of exposed film, so it felt psychologically a lot lighter.

At the top of the last rise beyond the pines, the faint line of shore at Badachro showed beyond Gairloch and long squat cottages and houses showed off-white in the dusk with dormer windows lighted. Were folk going to bed? I asked two young men to direct me to apartments—the lady, out! Next door, none available! Another—same reason! Up the lane—again, no success! Nine houses! The hotel 'full up'! Ten houses, until it was too dark to see my way from house to house. A young lady tried to help me but of no avail so I went hungry, tired and cold, after the hot day, and sat hunched up in the telephone kiosk and placed my stick to keep the door ajar to prevent my suffocation. I remembered the lady had said at Aultbea "Please don't travel on Sunday, the rest will do you good!" It is of course the custom of the people to discourage tourists breaking the peace of the Sabbath by going from place to place.

I got cramped and ravenous, so decided, since I knew the road well, to struggle on to Carn Dearg youth hostel, another 2½ miles further on, which I reached like a battered tramp steamer limping into port at 10 o'clock—a wiser man.

After a good meal plus attention to my blisters and a little chat with the hostellers, it was time to retire. I was ready, at the end of a day to remember.

11 *The Artist of Gairloch*

I FELT by now like Marco Polo seeing rare sights and hearing strange tales and leaving the hostel—a one-time architect's home—on the shoulder of the loch, with its bird house fixed to the tree by the lawn more sand than grass, I set off to find John Fielder, the artist of the peninsula at Big Sand. I couldn't spare another walking day and had decided to call the visitation off as John had been exhibiting at Edinburgh and folk said he hadn't returned. Not more than five miles had I gone when an old car halted. "Jump in," a voice said. "I'm taking you back and I'll return you here tomorrow to start off again, how's that?" I agreed and John (who had returned) had me soon to his old crofter's cottage near the salmon fishery at Big Sand.

John Fielder has an American wife Jane, with their son David, who live in an old stone cottage with two rooms down and two in the roof. By his initiative and a friend's help, from this remotest house in the area, they have made a nice comfortable place a quarter of a mile from the shore steep down a gully where salmon fishery nets hang on a drying gantry. Away across Gairloch, south-east, they can see the mountains of Torridon, and westwards the setting sun and the sea from the little headland, an artist's paradise.

Fielder has left his home near Barnsley, the colliery area, to be amongst the sublimest scenery in Scotland. He and I met first when he had charge of the youth hostel and seeing my two cameras he sensed I was a fanatic in photography, and myself seeing a magnificent array of pictures displayed on the hostel walls, I enquired who the artist could be. "Who do you think?" he asked. Looking in the dark eyes of a fierce face, I ventured, *"You!"* "Right man!" he flashed, as we both grasped each other's hands, and have become fast friends ever since 1967.

He is gradually acquiring the knowledge of how to live

frugally by eating shore foods which replace the more sophisticated dietary items like cabbage and other greens, particularly relishing blue-stalks of the mushroom family. Jane and John know the value of simple living, for to obtain water a journey to a communal stand-pipe is necessary, fetching two buckets per journey, and not a drop used unnecessarily. We had our main meal together where I was specially honoured by having potatoes and peas from his own 'lazy-bed' garden.

John showed me the effects of sheep ravaging peas, cabbages and carrots after some foolish tourist had 'looked in' during their absence and left the gate open. He was furious. I was astonished at the marvellous produce he had grown by using the ditched method of lazy-bed working, which drains the land from excess water yet leaves sufficient to induce growth in dry seasons. For fertilization he thickly spreads both seaweed and sheep dung amongst the peaty earth, and as he turned the potatoes from his plot, I recalled seeing a crofter in the Outer Hebrides, who said, "Aren't they lovely?" as he opened his cupped hands to reveal his clean beautiful potatoes newly dug with grains of sand sparkling on their skins.

Night came too soon when the Fielders made a dual purpose visit to a neighbouring crofter's cottage for they had promised the old lady and her daughter they should see their young baby David, and I should see the interior of a real Highland cottage. The inky blackness of night was darker than a Rembrandt's interior, and only by closely following feet showing in the glow of a torch light did I manage that squelchy, tussocky quarter of a mile over the rough land. It was next morning that we saw the thatched roof, the few coals, and the peat stack, but for the present we entered after a knock, to see the old lady seated by the fire under a large canopy. The peat glowed as flames circled the large kettle, always 'on the go' for pot washing, and tea, soon brewing to enliven our chatter.

About food, this in the old days was of little variety and long journeys afoot had to be made to the shop to fetch it, except what could be found by the shore or by fishing. I once had been fishing with a Hebridean friend and by his skill and my luck we caught so many as to be able to distribute them to neighbours.

I simply detest cleaning fish before cooking, so Mrs MacKinnon prepared and cooked a superb evening meal for a good number of hostellers and as a special treat gave me the water they were steamed in, calling it 'soup'. I shuddered when she said "Drink it, it will be good for you." No envious eyes watched me slowly imbibe that delicious soup after she had salted and peppered it, and next time I'm lucky, I'll prepare some more and share it. It's *super.*

From simple ingredients, the Scottish housewives are so adept they can prepare some tasty and nourishing foods, and from oats, potatoes, raisins, sheep carcasses and fish, it is exciting to see what next is being served up—maybe haggis!

A great *bonhomie* existed in the old days, she said, for anyone with a pony would gladly bring things from the shop to save others long and wearying journeys in bad weather.

When folk are ill, they are *ill,* there is no malingering, and doctors are not fetched out unless necessary to cross boggy terrain. The old lady said her sister needed hospital treatment, just after the first world war, and had to be carried over rough ground to the distant road, and then by rough road to Achnasheen railway station, next by train to Inverness, and lastly by road to the hospital. Folk never grumbled about the hardships and agonies, and were, as now, ever ready to help each other.

These days motor ambulances and better roads have been the means of preventing many serious troubles, by speeding patients to hospital before dangerous situations occur, and folk are grateful. Yet there are sudden causes of illness or agony which have to receive more immediate attention, yet do not warrant a long journey to cure.

A friend of mine once developed a raging toothache and cycled for attention from a semi-retired dentist. The dentist's wife ushered him into an outshot veranda and offered him a deep armchair, telling him to wait until her husband's arrival. Eventually a boiler-suited fellow strolled in, asking what was the trouble and then went to another apartment. My friend rose to follow. "Sit where you are, man, I'm coming," the man called, as he fetched from a small box situated amongst flower pots and plants the equipment he needed, and in a jiffy the trouble was over! There is no room in the Highlands for the squeamish, as fillings were seldom undertaken in the old days.

As we talked, the daughter was told by her mother to stoke up to keep the house warm for the baby, then every nook became aglow with yellow light.

"Why do you burn coal so much when peat is so cheap?" I asked.

"Well," she said, "it's no use getting much peat in heaps, for the tourists take it as a souvenir, or pilfer it for their own use, so we use coal, which comes by puffer in 100-ton loads to Gairloch, and then by lorry as near to the house that can be managed."

There was so much warmth and light from the iron grating beneath the canopy that the electric light wasn't necessary, for the white plastered walls set off every piece of furniture, whilst the thick walls and heavy thatch kept out the cold air from the night outside. I took a photo of the old lady with John and Jane's bairn, and we were off, back again on that fearsome stretch in inky blackness save for the torch, and arrived safely.

John Fielder, this artist-poet, stocky, swarthy, with penetrating eyes, stands squarely, often with his hands thrust in his trouser tops, thumbs outwards, looking formidable like a Freddy Trueman in duplicate. Words are few as from Dylan Thomas—'peat smoke' poetry. His eyes speak first, those of a detective. He ferrets out the life blood of a subject for his canvas and keeps line, tone, and colours to the minimum, giving great impact.

I have one or two of John's masterpieces, and when I yearn to return momentarily to the Highlands, I stand and look at a picture of some lone pines on the windswept moors and immediately I feel amongst the elements of wind and rain with the smells of pine and bracken in the air, and even more, I hear the roar of the distant sea, breaking over the rocks he doesn't show.

We said our goodbyes in the little crofter's cottage and Fielder the artist of Gairloch returned me to my trekking point of re-commencement. It was a tremendous wrench to part, but as soon as I'd slammed the door of his old car, he was off back to his easel, and myself to the long grind of walking alone.

12 *Magnificent Loch Maree*

I SET out with a will this morning, knowing I must be in accommodation before dark, for there is no more eerie landscape than that around Loch Maree hotel with its haunting tales of tragedy and escapement. *Scared?* Rubbish, but when darkness comes every yard unknown seems like ten. On past the cottages by the little bay, then by the sheltered church and finally by the harbour to the little pier. Sandy and his crew of three in the red-hulled fishing boat *True Love* would be out somewhere off Skye, later bringing in their catch of herring and white fish. I was once sea-sick in that boat, alarmingly, I had gone to take photographic records of 'men at work' but was completely disabled, yet feebly, learned that on that rolling sea they earned every penny of their wages, for I simply couldn't stand, let alone work.

Then by the shore cottages last of Gairloch, I saw the lobsterman John Macdonald, come up from his boat repairing, through the conifers high across the road to a rocky terrace to have his 'elevenses' to where he took me into his beautiful home, from which we looked down steeply to the harbour. From this, he sails to secret crannies for lobsters, where you or I would never dream of dropping down pots leaving their markers bobbing. "Aye, there's a good freemasonry between true fishermen who are locals, for they tell each other where best to plant their pots to get best catches." He 'white' fishes in good weather, but works close home in bad weather or in wintertime when it is dark until 10 a.m. and returns again soon in the afternoon. "Baits, man, the crabs like fresh ones whereas lobsters will accept stale baits, and as for what get in a pot," he said, "I once had an eel, a crab and an otter in the one pot."

Many times have I enquired how fish populated lochs high in the mountains, before humans incubated them in hatcheries and took them there from fish tanks. I was told here in Gairloch that some forms of flying beetles love to gorge themselves amongst fish spawn and consequently some fish eggs cling between the hairs on their bodies, and the insects flying to higher water dislodge them into the seemingly inaccessible waters.

Leaving the artist's paradise, the harbour, the pub, the post office and the lobster fisherman and his wife, my back soon turned on civilization and in half a mile huge deciduous trees and conifers were being thinned out by the noisy chain-saws. The brawny-armed 'fellers' seemed glad to have a word about their jobs, as did a telephone engineer working on his own, who allowed me to use his trowel to mortar some of the bricks in the road manhole.

Soon, I was so alone that cows and sheep wandered about the road, quite unconcerned about me. It seemed so much down to earth as I drank from the same prattling river as themselves, but upstream. Above the normal sound of water a distant hum indicated a generating station which apparently worked unattended, providing power for the national grid. Looking for the watercourse to turn the motors, I saw huge pipes greatly camouflaged that came from up the glen, bringing down a spate of water from Loch Bad-an-Sgalaig.

After a long struggle winding in and out, I reached the loch soon to be connected with another with a few idle rowing boats lying offshore. It seemed like the Garden of Eden, completely unspoiled with sheltering mountains all around and a late afternoon sun with brightly rimmed clouds surrounding their summits.

A footbridge crosses the outlet stream leading to a footpath away to a delectable 'beyond' which ultimately leads to the distant sea. Here is a rambler's paradise at any season and with transport to this point, map-reading ability, and good conditions, this is the area for a few days' invigorating walking.

As yet the great thirteen miles Loch Maree, which had been hidden from the road by a mountain and high land, ultimately yielded a view after a three hours' trudge, providing a magnificent sight between trees at the end of the path from Poolewe!

There across the grey water, diffusedly reflecting the grey clouds amassing over the mountain range, stretching both ways as far as the eye could see, it looked eternal as from the beginnings of creation—yet in 1772 a chronicler reported findings of cannon barrels and grates founded in some works on the shore side near Letterewe. I was glad no spuming smoke and steam, or clutter of factories, were evident or likely to be, for if ever there would be a blot on the landscape surely this would despoil such a glorious panorama. Possibly the bog iron worked out, for there has been no evidence of works since 1800.

With this sublime scenery one side and huge shoulders of rock and bushes the other, with the one-track meandering road for my walking, my last mile suffused me with peace. I was glad for the holiday season to be over, for heaven knows what skirmishes of cars and caravans there have been in the past, at some of the worst angled and blind bends there are on any Scottish roads.

Somehow Dr Johnson's journeyings were to be envied, when with the sound of clopping hooves, folk would be warned in sufficient time to avoid accidents, but all the excitement of driving on formerly perilous roads is fast disappearing, now that the muffled roar of explosives indicates literal moving of mountains to straighten highways.

Soon the road became easier but yet more eerie in the fast-gathering dusk as I trod upon thick carpets of pine needles and after another day of exciting walking it was gladdening to see the stout stone gables of Loch Maree Hotel, where the management very kindly 'pushed me in' an already crowded place, sleeping in a vacated staff member's bedroom.

Before I left I was given a packed lunch to fortify me on my biggest day's stint yet—eighteen miles, and wet ones, for a sticky drizzle began and maintained its clammy company to the end. I was to see the first real weather identifiable with Scotland. Ugh! I 'battened down', anorak on and rain-hood over, but the stuff seemed to get in everywhere. It's no good, young man, I thought. 'You half expected this. Now make the best of it.' This part of Scotland is 'terrific' (I'm tired of saying superb, glorious, sublime and fantastic), for the wild hummocky boulders and bog rose and fell and the road with them yielding fresh stretches of water and the little islands dotting the huge loch. Large shoulders of rock were a façade to the fine mountains and here at one time when walking, I saw a dead stag just off the road, and a deer surveying the landscape a stone's-throw away—safe on the high ground. Slioch (3217 feet) lay like a reposing giant, head in the mist, way over the other side; I was thrilled in spite of the sticky going.

It was hardly 'lunch break' and feeling it better to shelter than to dilute my coffee with copious supplies of Scotch drizzle, I took the chance of sheltering in some road works contractors' huts. A chimney smoked; that would do fine to have a warm place. I knocked, and was admitted by a bearded office worker, an Irishman, who quickly assessed I was no vagrant. Introduced to four others, one being Ian, another office worker—junior member—a draughtsman engineer. They asked "Who are you?" "Hector, why are you doing this?" "When do you expect to finish?" So it went on, and an hour flew.

"So long, fellows, you've been very kind to me, but I must make Torridon youth hostel before dark." Off I shot on the muddy road, and 'had a go' with a pneumatic drill, making holes to receive explosives for blasting large rocks for easier moving.

"Who are you, young man?" asked the operator.

"Hector Kyme! What's your name?" In reply a big, dirty hand shot out and grasped mine like a bulldozer's grab. The fellow said "Hector, there's two of us." He took the 'dddddrill bbbback', but looked so much happier for a word with me, for his face shone above the rain-glistening beard to the furrowed brow joining the pair of glinting eyes which 'spat' resolution under the dark overhang of a huge sou'wester. Both his work and my walk needed an iron discipline to keep going, and soon the day's 'sorrow' separated us.

I had travelled before on the 'old' road but now came the 'new' these fellows just seen had recently constructed. It was marvellous at least for making the 'sparks fly', and before long I was near the loch end, 'finished'. Rain or no rain, I couldn't resist a photograph trying to catch the grandeur of a misty day in the Highlands and risked the damage water can do to a good camera.

At this end of Loch Maree, there is a gap between Slioch and Beinn a Mhuinidh (2231 feet), where with an experienced guide, one can pass between and have a grand day's walk or climb, but this day I was glad to see anyone to offset the loneliness of damp silence without seeking the eerie solitudes, when a gumbooted postman cyclist came to the end of his circuit. He delivered his mail and turned about, still with more to deliver round Kinlochewe. He spoke cheerily, and reminded me of another post worker, a postwoman, who resolutely went about in lonely places to distant hill-farms; it was wartime and a day of snow. She had reached one farm away in the hills and had yet another call to make at one even more remote place, but since the item for delivery was a weekly periodical, she left it to be handed on if the weather improved. The farmer didn't get his paper! The next delivery day, again with the weekly edition, conditions warranted a journey to the top farm, where on arrival she was castigated for not doing her duty. "We've never been without our week-end paper before, woman; do your duty." This woman had trampled miles to the farm in foul, wet and windy weather, without ever receiving thanks, or being offered a rest by the fire on cold days and never a cup of tea, then this man mentioned 'duty'.

"Man," she said, "I am not officially obliged to bring your paper if conditions are too bad to warrant me making the effort, and if you did your duty to see one of your able-bodied sons into the army, then I might have some encouragement to fight through the weather to oblige you. Good morning."

There were no more grumbles after that.

I had reached Kinlochewe, topped my iron rations, posted a couple of letters, had a snack and 'cuppa', deciding on this dismal afternoon to make the rest of the journey without a halt: eight long miles before dark! Taking leave of the small, pleasant, weeping village between Loch Maree and Glen Docherty at a T junction, I set off down Torridon with great determination to do my loneliest walk yet, and on such a dismal day, then with the resolution of a test cricketer fast bowler—who licks his fingers before hurling down a snorter

—I got into a rhythmic striding I felt I could maintain and soon passed all traces of habitations and forged on between six-foot deer fences surrounding the pine plantations. Gloomy and eerie aren't the words—there is a claustrophobic feeling in Torridon any time, but the heavy clouds surrounding the bases of the mountains made it a day for old-time plundering of cattle, deer or sheep.

I looked periodically at my 'Newfield' watch, giving myself $2\frac{1}{2}$ miles to each hour at a guess and strove on to gain time, for that glen in the dark is unthinkable. A few vehicles strangely enough came meeting me as if fleeing from the Devil's dungeon and were gone in the mist. Yet the experience to me was marvellous to see this wild glen in gloom. I have seen it many times with shining screes and vast flanks dark and brooding, a challenge to the spirit as one gets older, and now my one desire was to see the gable of Torridon youth hostel in the dark pines.

The brawl of the river kept me company as I passed that suberb glen into the moorland by Loch Clair between Sgùrr-Dubh and Càrn Breac and keeping ahead with unflagging rhythm, like the boat race victors, I recognized that forbidding giant Liathach (3456 feet), too proud to show his head. Cheers! I will make it, and now, as I was close to the precipitous face of the mountain, I knew the hostel must be near, and peering through the beads of mingled drizzle and sweat on my eyelashes I looked for the forlorn pines. The mist would not yield. Is it? I walked on a hundred yards and more It is, a light! There at last reassurance, I knew it well, the homely glow of the welcoming light in a crowded hostel—the gloomy day had brought darkness ominously sooner by an hour. I still see that lighted window like a harbour beacon guiding a small vessel into dock, after walking eighteen miles from Loch Maree Hotel.

13 *The Spell of the West*

As I entered the back door of the hostel, so much row came from the dining-room no one heard me, so I placed my soaked clothing on the racks near the hot stove and entered the lions' den. There were three Americans, one being the personification of Abraham Lincoln, and sundry other folk of clans and countries—but talk of the Tower of Babel, this was it indeed. I could scarcely make myself heard. I was ravenous and needed a seat, but soon a meal of fried haddock, potatoes and rice was put before me, a meal which made me shudder, but I ate it.

Soon after, 'Abraham', who looked interested in my appearance, asked where I had been and where making for. "Really!" Somehow the row ceased and I was questioned: did I sing or whistle? We started with the 'Mingulay Boat Song', accompanied by a first-rate guitarist who possessed a rich baritone voice. Soon though, being tired, I went to bed.

First up, and for breakfast, a cup of tea and a very small pie, no more. Food had run short with so many guests using the hostel, due to bad weather dissuading camping. On that frugal meal I set out three miles to Torridon village amidst magnificent scenery, but my scenic appetite was secondary to my physical one.

The narrow valley with Liathach's overpowering height looked magnificent after the day of rain, and was now in bright sunshine, while campers amongst the pines had started preparing a 'frizzle', the tantalizing aroma of which aggravated my intense hunger, but I pressed on to the village.

I passed the delectable road to Diabaig and soon was passing the tidiest little church and graveyard one could ever see, reverently maintained, and by the end of Upper Loch Torridon. Breakfast! I went to the first cottage and got showered by rain-bowed honeysuckle. "Och no bread, sorry," said the nice old lady. "Try Bay View, you'll get some there."

It needed a special effort to move on after having done three miles on an empty stomach and carrying my pack. A hundred yards ahead two men chattered, the older man having a dog moving off at my approach.

"Nice morning sir, which is Bay View please?"

Without moving round the stocky 45-ish fellow indicated the house "There," directing his thumb over his shoulder, in which direction I went with equal brevity to a porch doorway. The garden long and beautiful terminated at a dwelling well maintained and painted. I quietly knocked, but the lady must have seen me coming, and I'm sure she wondered who this could be so early, as the door opened. Rather embarrassed I made my plea—didn't want to trouble her—"And could I please have extra food and drink for my day's journey, I would be grateful?" She admitted me, saying "I will give you a coffee first to be going on with, please sit there." 'There' was a seat at a nice dining table under which I had scarcely put my feet when the coffee arrived, immediately followed by a plate full of bacon, eggs, tomato and sausage. This was a miracle indeed. However I had not had time to observe a second seating at the table where the lady placed the meal, when the broad-shouldered 'thumb indicator' sat opposite the plate, nodding to me, before he began to do justice to the feast.

"Good morning, I've seen you before haven't I?" I said.

"Och aye."

We had scarcely broken the ice when Mrs Mackenzie brought in a second plate as amply festooned as the first. After I had thanked her I began to do justice to her culinary arts. As we two men feasted, Mr Mackenzie, who proved not so taciturn as at first appeared, discussed with me what each did as an occupation. He is a self-trained man who works at the local hotel, doing all the allied trades classified under building construction. As for apprenticeship, he used 'do it yourself' books, and besides saving the hotel management much capital and inconvenience, he gains for himself much self-satisfaction.

After rising he has a snack, goes to the hotel to start things moving and then returns for breakfast. Probably his wife should have breakfasted with him, but I found later Mrs Mackenzie had busied herself with packing some food for me for my journey while 'the men gossiped'. Her husband returned to work after shaking hands, then I spruced up and felt tidier after the stickiness of the previous day.

"Mrs Mackenzie," I said, "I'm ready to go, but not before I have tried to recompense you for all your kindness and at some inconvenience. How much am I in your debt—as I am very grateful to you?"

We looked each other in the face, then after our eyes filled she said quietly, "Nothing, it's my birthday." I vow she looked ten years younger than her real age, and I had been at a birthday party I'll never forget.

Full of pep up the hill I went past the hotel and the Highland Cattle by the compound gate, when a yell like the night before made me look round. It grew louder until the Land-Rover passed, of course, the youngsters of the hostel were journeying the lazy way and cheering me on.

On top of the hill, looking all around is beyond superlatives. Give me a rowing boat and a line, some art materials, a job at the hotel, an old cottage in the village and Dora, my wife, to humour me; we could live there for ever. To see the dawn and the sunset over the snow-capped mountains, to watch the tides ebb and flow in the Upper Loch Torridon, to natter with nice people and to give help to strangers, must surely be the ultimate of happiness. There, as I 'flogged' myself to make headway, was the most fantastic scenery everywhere—the great sea loch and distant Torridon Glen behind, and before me the huge abrupt face of Ben Shieldaig (1691 feet) rising straight up from sea level. I felt small. If Scotland were a poem, surely hereabouts would be the most precious stanza of all—Shieldaig.

I lingered on this section of the journey to soak in the beauty, for there is no comparable place on earth surely where not a breath stirs, nor where the cottages nestle as closely, garbed in their several bright colour washes, nor where the waters languidly lap the little jetty and its unmanned boat: my first visit was in rain, but now in sunshine, what a transformation—a gem of purest ray serene! I left the Rip Van Winkles asleep and struck off up through Glen

Shieldaig forest, listening to the stream as it tumbled and flashed, joyously meeting the sea.

Resisting the road turn to the right towards Applecross—for on that precipitous road in the making is the finest scene outside of heaven—I paced up over a giant's toe of 350 feet and boiling in the afternoon heat, eventually reached the summit road, seeing the vast panorama of mountains of Wester Ross-shire. Judging from the map and the view itself, surely there are few roads in Britain with such splendour to see from a car. For me it was worth all the sweat.

I coasted down the dark, shadowy hillside now in evening glow, heading for Kishorn, my rendezvous, and of all the remarkable shapes of mountains I have ever seen is Beinn Bhan (2936 feet), for it is tortuous in outline and fearsome in appearance. A huge concave curve in its mass is symbolic of a devil's cauldron, with a huge landslip held inside; no wonder our ancestors were afraid of such sinister masses when lightnings and thunders played about their summits.

I tried to stay at the farm in the valley bottom; no one about! On I 'flogged' on advice given at a forester's house to stay at Friday's.

"Won't the gentleman be insulted when I ask if he is Mr Friday?"

"No, everybody knows him as that."

After two weary miles all I was greeted by at the large house surrounded by large, dark trees was a large, old dog and cat. It was Thursday. 'Friday' was out!

A motorist, the next and only person I saw, said, "Go back on the road by the 'big board' and my husband and I will board you." I dragged my tired limbs another three-quarters of an hour and passed the sign to Applecross which I couldn't read, it was so dark, and then stood under a coach house doorway to await the car's return. It was now cold; I poured out my last hot drink, when on came some headlights. They're here! I threw the coffee away, flask pushed in the haversack, and stood, awaiting for the car to halt—I was wrong, it was someone else. Cold and hungry, I waited in absolute gloom for ages, then Friday's daughter, Mrs Donald Mackenzie, pulled up and finally landed me in the old mill house where

I received superb hospitality and heard some fine local history.

Mr and Mrs Donald Russel (or 'Donny' Russel) are in fact the Mackenzies, and since so many folk have such a surname, they are called Russel after his birthplace. His wife also was a Mackenzie before her marriage, and her father was given the Christian name Friday to differentiate between him and another with the same first name. There are three Donald Mackenzies, so the postman has to have some special coding to prevent some probably embarrassing mistakes.

As for the huge, ominous notice-board by the end of Loch Kishorn, it warns all road traffic users that drivers are to be experienced (and vehicles in sound condition implied) before the road to Applecross is taken. This road, made in 1804-08 climbs 2054 feet and extends for twelve miles. On it are dreadful hairpin bends and perilously steep portions, but the views from this the highest roadway in Britain are breathtaking and the village when reached claims the title of the most beautiful in Scotland.

To bed.

14 *Let it Rain*

DONNY 'Russel' works in the near 3000-foot mountains as deer stalker, maintaining fences to prevent herds from damaging young trees. Formerly creatures of the woods, they could hide from their enemies. Now the deer seek high pasturage in the mountains far from foes but mainly to avoid midges and flies.

The stalker told me, one day he saw in a hollow high in the hills a dozen unusually placed deer, standing in a circle with one in the middle dancing. Using his binoculars he noticed after a time the 'dancer' changed places with one in the outer ring which took up the ritual. He had never seen or heard of such an incident before, and approached the animals to discover that changing places occurred several times before they scattered. On looking in this arena he found an adder which they had taken dangerous turns to destroy in order to be safe from a mortal enemy.

On another occasion, a dog fox which had been caught had a piece of bark in which were six dead mice placed in grass to prevent loss as he went to his brood of six cubs; so there this lithe fellow has always plenty of interest in his lonely work. I asked him about the weather as I had to go to the nearest bank having only four pounds cash for any lodgings over the weekend. He informed me "Lochcarron village; and the weather will be poor."

Off again. Mrs 'Donny' Mackenzie kindly took me by car to the spot where she first saw me and waved "Goodbye", then on past the youth hostel and the post office and the sheltering Belgian girls with blackberry-stained fingers, on into a worsening drizzle, until a wayside hut sheltering two woodmen gave me cheerful respite. It was so wet these fellows couldn't spread their fertilizers round the bases of saplings, plant saplings, or protect saplings, it was so dreary.

"Why do you work here instead of a city with chance of greater remuneration?" I asked these intelligent men.

"Because we prefer the expanses of sea, mountain and forest, even on a day like this, than to be cooped up in a dreary office or large factory with clanging rows and smelly chemics; the open life for us!"

Too soon I battened down my hatches, showing only my face, and strode out into the rain which blew the more unpleasantly as I climbed over yet another giant's toe—a high ridge overlooking Loch Carron. It seemed like a Himalayan monsoon as I squelched towards the chimney-smoking village; seeing only one semblance of humanity as a huge umbrella bobbed over a pair of legs.

Got my cash, and left a 'deposit'—a huge pool of water from my soaking anorak spreading over the bank floor.

Fancy, wet through after five miles. I struck out for the next village, another three miles with rain descending like steel wire making road pools dance in frenzy and the stream from under the bridge careering like a mad horse swaying blackberry fronds and twigs in its frothy swirls.

Mountain streams raced down white with foam like mares' tails, and sheets of water seemed graced with Olympic circles as rings from raindrops laced each other in this incessant deluge. Enough, at Strathcarron I tried one house after another for accommodation, unsuccessfully, and partly dried out clothes in the hotel gas oven while John provided me with a welcome snack. Still wet, I went on the new road built to avoid the use of ferries over Strome—eight miles to Achmore.

This road runs parallel with one of the most beautiful railways in the world and never more beautiful than on this evening—the sun came out. The great rocks shone in wetness, and cataracts raced down into the loch, while mountain summits towered above the cloaks of mist about their steaming flanks. They seemed like resting animals sweating after the chase. I at last agreed with Ruskin, "there is no such thing as bad weather, it is good for something", and what more wonderful than to see the shimmering evening light on the loch with the houses I had passed on the other side one by one showing their lighted windows and dark silhouettes.

The massive rocks reared, encased in some places with

protective netting as safeguards against falling boulders and at one place so near to the water that road and railway run within feet of each other, both protected by a Swiss-type concrete tunnel, a masterpiece of functional designing. At each end there are what could have been plain concrete spandrels, but a foreman had the excellent idea of decorating the landward end with incised moulding showing animals native to Scotland, and on the seaward approach, all manner of fish and birds native to the west coast. It is undoubtedly the best piece of concrete sculpting I have seen.

Still wet after the day's effort, before climbing the 'hill difficulty' named by local folk, I sat in the gathering darkness and poured out my flask contents and watched a car's headlights gradually approach me. After an age, it stopped, when a voice shouted, "Hello Hector, how are you? You've done well; got any digs?"

"Don't know you, sir, who are you?"

"Ian Campbell. Remember the draughtsman in the office by Loch Maree?"

"Yes of course!" I nearly snatched his hand off!

"Can I give you a lift or take your pack?" he asked.

"Not on your life, we're good company now and don't separate!"

Ian went home and found me superb lodgings, returning to meet me as I struggled for about an hour up the long lonely road between giant pines. He had arranged everything at Mrs Chisholm's house where she provided excellent fare and washed and dried my soggy clothes; and, thank heavens though for plastic bags, my change was dry as snuff.

Leaving the Campbells' and Chisholms' community on a glorious morning I was soon shouldering away through a herd of escaped cows on the narrow road, one of the most magnificent I have ever seen, high above Plockton and Loch Carron looking over towards Skye and Applecross. *Sea Sprite,* Prince Charles's yacht he sailed when at Gordonstoun, lay at anchor amongst others down in Plockton bay, with little white houses surrounding the semi-circle of deep blue. It was indeed the renowned place for artists, bathed in sunshine, idling amongst its gardens of pampas grass, palms and flowers.

As if like a matron in charge of the area, Duncraig Castle

stood prominently high over the loch edge, being a college for domestic science trainees, where young ladies entering the bold archway are admonished in words chiselled in the stones —*Fear God, work hard, be honest.*

Only a short sea trip away lies the sister village of Applecross, also warmed by the Gulf Stream, where in the old days monks grew fruit in the orchards to dispatch to the islands. To evangelize the purchasers of fruit, the monks used to stick paper crosses on the sunnier side of each apple, which as it grew the skin only reddened where fully exposed, and on the removal of the paper, a bleached cross remained to remind folk of Christ's sacrifice, hence the village name of Applecross.

Unable to get food requirements or iron rations in the crowded shop full of Dutch tourists, I set off hopefully to Kyle, but the shops were closed.

The sublimest evening walk one could think of is the one from Plockton to Kyle of Lochalsh by the railway side —don't trespass—it was magnificent with the sombre peaks of the Cuillins ever deepening in colour as night came on, and should artists wish to try other sites than Plockton, the little hamlets of Durinish, Drumbuie, and Erbusaig should please the most fastidious.

Finally, scrambling up the bridge wall like Joe Brown, after a long day, I was soon enjoying a fine stew with two young Americans in the old schoolhouse youth hostel.

15 *Over the Sea to Skye*

If you can see Skye it's going to rain,
If you can't see Skye it's raining.

"KYLE of Lochalsh, Sunday, little breakfast, unable to buy food, hope to manage eight miles to Broadford in the strength of resolution."

The view from the hostel on the outskirts looking across to Skye is fantastic: I think of the Cuillins from here as like a pow-wow of Indians seated under the wigwam of Heaven, the drifting clouds from their summits being the whiffs of smoke from their pipes. I waited a long, hungry time for the first ferry to cross the narrow Kyle to Kyleakin (pronounced Kyle-akin not Kyleeekin) and still couldn't get food, so set off in the drizzle leaving this delectable area, the spearhead of a probable new road bridge to eliminate the use of ferries —a terrible bottleneck in the holiday season.

At Kyleakin near the lighthouse just across is the former residence of the author of *Ring of Bright Water*, and way down the kyle at Loch Duich is the famous Eilean Donan Castle, in fact, if Giant Atlas scored a circle with a radius of twenty miles from Kyleakin as centre, one would not excel anywhere such a glorious region of beauty.

I left the little fishing fleet silently moored near the castle ruin and ambled past the mountain Sgurr-na-Coinnich from whose flanks, I once saw, all simultaneously, deer, herons and seals. Blackberries 'kept the wolf at bay', but yet I grew weaker until my legs sank beneath me and lay with my head in the strap harness. I was too limp to continue.

Over an hour afterwards the chilly rain wakened me and sheer endeavour took me to a former hostel warden's house where in half an hour I was myself again through her ready kindness. Soon I ambled into Broadford past the pool in the stream where a huge salmon could neither go up nor down—trapped for the greedy, I couldn't release it—and went on past the hay drooping over a fence drying between showers waiting for a long spell of fine weather before being stooked finally over the three-way pyramid for winter feed.

Still before hostel opening time I looked over the bridge where large eels wriggled about waiting for morsels from 'heaven', well at least high above from the parapet, when a thin-faced middle-aged lady wearing wellingtons decided I would be a ready listener to her pent-up wrath. She took out the safety valve and steamed ahead, giving a diatribe regarding the disgraceful conduct of some caravanners who pull into a field without permission, leave all their rubbish and filth, plus plastic bags which choke animals, never pay anything and use objectionable language when addressed.

'In dock', the youth hostel wardens, Mr and Mrs Taylor, were fine in providing for my next day's seventeen-mile journey, and in spite of all their commitments I found delightful little extras I never asked for—at no charge—and being up by 7 o'clock was off before many hostellers had ceased snoring.

Leaving Broadford, setting out near the old pier, I had soon passed the doctor's boat I once rowed, waved to the Sutherland's with whom I once stayed enjoyably, past the fire-ravaged café we often dined in and now thankfully repaired. Then out on the moorland road to Armadale determined to do six miles without a halt, I was soon passing the reedy pools where water lillies in summer float like full-sailed yachts. I was in a complete world of my own, a lonely figure seeing no one for an hour and thrilled to see again across to Loch Hourn the Devil's Loch all grey and grim, no misnomer. The old lighthouse at Isle Ornsay grimly guarded the promontory at one of the most magnificent scenic situations of my marathon—misty and moody—not like the last time, when clouds in sunshine canopied the dappled pools and sand where sheep nibbled turf down to the seaweed crops.

The old store house now silent after ten years, where one could once get a dozen candles, a sack of corn, a bottle of whisky or a suit of clothes, stood solemnly near the empty pier that too was once busy—but now the trade has moved with the coming of road transport.

Last time at the cottage nearest the lighthouse I patted a collie dog which had a nasty limp. She was sorry for herself, no wonder by reason of the thousands of bottles washed ashore and many broken—she had been badly cut. Her owner said how the refuse floats down from the Kyles into the slack water of Isle Ornsay disfiguring an otherwise delightful shore.

I halted after a satisfying burst from Broadford and was asked by a kind doctor and his wife to 'jump in' for the rest of the journey. "No, thank you." Indeed when I explained they seemed delighted in my 'send off' for retirement.

Passing the crofters' cottages close by the long ditches from which peat had been dug, they had settled down for winter with piled fuel near the doors, and hay stooked and tethered.

The road to Ord still wore a ribbon of grass showing through tarmac indicative of little use; yet what stupendous sunsets are seen from the village looking towards the Cuillins. There, the clustered mountains with the dominant Bla Bheinn (3042 feet), seemed like a school of children with their headmaster telling them to "get down to it and don't get your heads into the clouds".

Next Knock Castle, twelfth century, grim and ruined, recalled the day when my wife and I sat having a snack, when an over-enthusiastic sheepdog rounding up some strays jumped between us over our spread. But today only a few dead foxgloves served as a reminder of that sunny day. The old free church and schoolhouse, relic of the age when folk desired education before compulsion, still stood serene, and high off the road functioned little Teangue post office and shop where Alex and Margaret MacKinnon replenished my supplies and fêted me royally to speed me on my way to the awaiting *Clansman* at Armadale.

Their neighbour, Donald Macdonald, an Australian, has reversed the trend of emigration and now owns the croft and cottage, an inheritance from his athletic uncle who won a bronze medal for wrestling in 1924. Next in the distance the sound of children from Ferrin Donald School (Donald's Land) indicated playtime, and some observant youngsters wondered what I was doing and gasped "as far as that?" The trend of movement of families from Skye to the mainland is indicated by the schools which have closed; now only one functions in the area where there were six.

Away across the Sound of Sleat (Slate) I could see the hamlet of Airor in Knoydart, completely isolated on the mainland coast, its link with the outside world being Ian Macdonald's boat, used when he fetches goods from Alex and Margaret's store and to gather news.

By now I was able to slacken my pace and chatted a few moments with telephone engineers repairing the ravages of rodents still keen of a diet of plastic insulations. We were between the tree-lined road where once a motor cyclist, failing to negotiate a bend in the road, killed himself on the rocky shoulder. I must have been a little earlier than the hour the tragedy happened, otherwise a tall ghostly fellow, wearing a bloodstained head bandage and an oilskin coat, would have silently walked alongside me to Armadale.

At last, after seventeen miles, the awaiting *Clansman* ensured a safe retreat for me from further ghostly episodes. The road was as silent as death, and again had it been night-time, undoubtedly I would have heard familiar sounds of swishing wheels and clopping hooves in gallop, culminating in screams from the young lady lover who with her coachman friend had met untimely death on another bend. It was by the site of the old Armadale Castle in the old days that those two romantics had taken an unauthorized spin and in their haste to get away quickly met their doom.

At last I boarded the *Clansman* and left this fantastic Skye charged with beauty, romance and legend and sought refuge in the engine room in the bowels of this immaculate ship. The bells rang, the levers switched, the log books were entered, the medal-ribboned captain scrutinized the entries confirmed them, and by a trice we were the six miles' journey accomplished entering Mallaig harbour at the end of the road to the isles.

16 *On the Road to the Isles*

MALLAIG is both the terminus for the railway on a magnicent line and also for many superb sails to the outer isles.

One August day my wife and I went on a mail boat run a short trip into Loch Nevis. There were on the prow, fastened to the little mast, three bags of coal I assumed were for delivery; eventualities proved they were to hold the prow down.

Outside the harbour it was frightening and nothing short of miraculous how we got round the Sgurr of Eilean. Some passengers were scared and went below deck, while one was thrown off a seat to the deck. I frequently looked in the face of the pilot who showed fearless calm, and sailed us through wallowing seas first poised high and next in a deep trough, spray dousing our faces if we looked over the gunwale.

By skilful use of rudder and engine we were returned to harbour where I asked our steersman, "Are there times when you cannot make scheduled journeys sir?"

"Only when it's rough!"

To avoid such trips to an otherwise inaccessible farm, with cattle, two brothers decided to make a mile-long track by smashing rocks and digging out on the steep, frightening mountain slope. Ironically, after the completion of this safer journey, locally called the Burma road, one brother was drowned.

From Mallaig itself or the neighbouring heights, the scenery is superb, especially towards the Cuillins. It also possesses a kipper factory which when dispensing offal into the sea, causes thousands of gulls to wheel, dive and screech incessantly, and he is a brave man who dare walk in the vicinity wearing a new hat, which would be a target hit with unerring accuracy from disrespectful birds.

My fine hosts at Mallaig, Angus Macdonald and his wife,

having dealt with accommodation problems further en route, had phoned a Gleann Mama farm that I was coming. I thus set out into a fierce wind and drizzle, when instead of Eigg and Rhum being inviting islands for exploration, they looked like grim submarines low on the water.

Up and down and round about past Loch Morar when no monster peered from the deepest lake in all Europe, on by the tidy white sands and the viewpoint for the finest sunsets of a life-time, where only the dark savage rocks scattered the sandy wastes. I struggled on, every stride an effort; I felt this could be my lot when planning the venture, but it was little use waiting for the wind to drop on this open stretch. I couldn't get liquid and became dehydrated. A—million—and —more—*strides*!! Arisaig—the hotel—the kindly proprietress (I phoned later to Mrs Macdonald, in the evening, I had 'made it' finely by her kindness). Only once again in all my journeys did this recur, unavoidably on a long stretch when short of 'fuel'. On strenuous days my coffee always contained a dash of salt for energy.

In the shelter of a ravine, the wind lessened where I felt fine, when a voice called "Well, we've looked all over for you, how are you?"

"Fine, mighty fine."

The Barghes from near home gave me a great fillip and took more exposed films back. I was relieved they had not seen me an hour before or they would have thought "This is the end—he's dying"!

Soon into evening past a fine stone-built farm and cottages, a kind fellow asked where I was to stay the night, and being asked if I could ring up, he said "Leave it to me" and would take no money.

Down between dark, dank foliage by Loch Nan Uamh, the sombre black waters reflected the silvery sky, pierced at intervals by reflections of mountains, the scene appearing like a Norwegian fiord. At last the reassurance that my gruelling task was almost over as my solitary footsteps rang with ghostly echoes under the railway arches, then after a stiff rise the light of the farmhouse revealed the home of my fine hosts the 'Shepherds—The Macinnes'.

17 *The Grand Detour*

THE sheep were still feeding with their rears to the wind, even though deer were still on top of the mountains behind Shepherd Macinnes's farm as I looked through his field glasses. His three sheepdogs waited commands ready to be rounding up his flock with other sheep, as all the farmers assist in the various projects, each man's sheep being identifiable by dye markings.

Meandering amongst the high mountains near the railroad a sense of claustrophobia gripped me as I passed the Black Loch which looks like the Devil's inkwell. I had been told specially to see an old man down at the foot of a deep glen by Loch Ailort—and without caution passed through a rusty iron gateway towards a rusty-roofed cottage far down a winding path. It was an unwise move—I had passed a warning sign 'Beware of the Bull'.

The old man and his sheepdog, Lassie, I saw were coming up the hill to fetch the paper put under a stone.

"What's your name? How old are you?"

"Hector Kyme. How old do you consider me, my friend?"

"Your name's mine. I'm Ronnie MacEachen, which means *Mac*—son, and *Eachen*—Hector. The son of Hector in Gaelic. You're 60!"

"Good, I feel that."

I felt to have shed five years in about three weeks. Ronnie lived with his stone-deaf, aged sister in the lost hamlet, for all the other cottages were in complete ruin.

"Aye, the postie in the old days had nae motor-van, only a horse which carried him and two saddlebags for mail."

"Och aye, I had trouble once as a wee laddie, a neighbour's disagreeable dog bit me, then the old woman said I would be all right in a few days after treating my injury with Zambuck ointment, and sure enough I was."

We Hectors parted. I watched him slowly descend to his silent home and then took to the road leaving the familiar Fort William direction, to explore new country by Moidart and Strontian. I had hardly begun when a voice shouted "Come and have a break with us, friend" and soon I was in the home of Mr and Mrs Thomas Gillan. This council worker had seen me at the farm, since he was taking his own two boys and the two sons of the Macinnes family to school, a taxi service he fulfils officially.

He took me outside to show the activities of the now busy shepherds and dogs amongst the sheep, moving like a drifting cloud on the mountain-tops as sorting exercises continued. He said amongst them was an old retired shepherd who could not leave the job alone, and would neither accept the fact of being of no further use. Then Thomas gave demonstrations of his two dogs paying instant obedience to commands. The family live by the railway halt at Lochailort and to stop trains in darkness intending passengers have to wave a lantern to notify drivers to halt. No more talking!

The Gillans saw me off, not before tempting me to "have a lift on the way", on the grand new road following the loch, in three distinct reaches, like Ullswater: but whereas Ullswater embraces the sky, Loch Ailort grasps the heavens. I felt like a Roman legionary striding over the new thoroughfare which has opened up this grand area wonderful to the scenic lover, the naturalist and the geologist.

Hereabout explosives and bulldozers have revealed wonderful examples of stratification, and from mountain heights magnificent views can be had of the outer isles. Some say this is the finest scenic area of Scotland; I wouldn't dispute this in spite of hanging mists, restricting my view.

Asking how soon would I see Glenuig Inn, the youngest lady of a foursome replied, 'The green one will tell you." They were Belgians—one dressed in green—who can't resist the opposite extremes from their own flat country and come here annually.

Passed the night in the packed Glenuig Inn where all were sociable, and set out early, passing the post office down the garden with a stream passing through, and hens strutting round the door, then strove over another giant's 'toe', not inappropriately, for I would pass near Ardtoe, Shielfoot, and through Blain.

It was obvious why Bonnie Prince Charlie escaped by Loch Shiel into the Moidart area for wild scenery of mountain, moor, and marsh, bushes, brambles and bracken, afforded splendid camouflage. Mountains and streams and lowland farms made superb vistas; and from a historic angle the 'Seven men of Moidart' which are trees planted by *eight* stalwart men, sworn to assist Charles Stuart, but one defected and his tree died, so now there are seven.

For the energetic, Rois Bheinn (2895 feet) and Druim Fiaclach (2852 feet) give unexampled sights of sea, lochs, islands and glens. A retired man envied me my energy and said he was exploring the neighbourhood for a house where he could end his days in the peace of this blissful region instead of the metropolis. I felt for him—his finances disallowed.

Then Acharacle and its school appeared with its contingent of children who split their sides at my failing attempts to say "Ach-ar-ac-cle".

Both Loch Shiel with its rainbow, and Loch Sunart are fantastic water stretches which must been seen to realize their vast beauty, for superlatives are inadequate to describe them. The aggravating temptation on this autumn morning was a rowing boat offshore, out of my depth to reach, so on I went to Strontian.

Nature had built up a mighty crescendo of magnificence at this place linked with the sources of atomic energy. So the misty sunset and the first white frost of approaching winter next day finally clinched my desire to see this huge peninsula again.

With dawn, the fierce rays of the powerful sun as it topped over the mountain range dispelled the white veil over the loch and replaced it with the brilliance of liquid silver. Now the narrow road as it ascended Glen Tarbert lay cluttered with idle giant earth-moving machinery, plus great patches of mud and rocky debris. Soon, though the new double-width road led over the top, giving breath-taking vistas of the mainland beyond Loch Linnhe; noticeable landmarks from this new angle were the Pap of Glencoe and its companion mountains forming the Pass. Way to the north the giant shadows of the Ardgour mountains close by Corran Ferry vied in magnificence with Ben Nevis plain as a sentinel thirteen miles away. I had added extra days to my journey, taking me further into November later, yet it had been worth every moment's effort to see the best Scotland has to offer.

18 *Roamin' in the Gloamin'*

CROSSED Corran Ferry and raced on to cross the famous one at Ballachulish before dark, to get an early start Sunday a.m. After four days with absolutely minimal traffic, now it was alarming to use the road from Fort William to Glencoe.

Called at grocers-cum-petrol pump, 'filled up' with iron rations. Customers, and the proprietress, eyed me over; "What are you doing, sir? ... Good for you!" and the shop owner thrust a few extras in my bag, the price offset by goodwill. Her son in charge of the one-time tailor's shop showed me the flamboyant royal coat of arms over the doorway, which referred to the patronage that the former tailor J. Macinnes possessed, in the days when the Prince of Wales, later Edward VII, came to have highland outfits.

The Prince, enjoying the canters on horseback, repeated his visits, which caused the tailor to grow conceited and increase his prices, whereby making it impossible for local people to patronize him. Princely orders, though welcome, were insufficient to maintain his business, and that is how the Camerons are in such a successful grocery establishment.

Out into the developing wind by the side of the choppy Loch Linnhe, a voice arrested me: "Hello there, young man, come and have a drink at the hotel. I have seen you many times and found what you're doing!"

"Teetotal, thanks!"

The man paced alongside. "Come on—give you a rest!"

"No thanks!"

"When you come through Kent, call on me, Ward, builder, and I'll take you every morning back where you leave off each day's stint."

(I endeavoured to later, but couldn't trace my well-wisher.) I was grateful, but pushed on for the last ferry.

Boats rocked at their moorings, as a sinister sky developed, and I chanced on the first sign of accommodation. A retired man stopped his last bit of hedge clipping to hear my enquiry. "I think you might stay here sir, I'll ask my wife first." A slight woman came, assessed my appearance in a flash, and called me into the strong crofter's cottage modified piecemeal to keep pace with modern trend.

Both Mr and Mrs Shaw belied their ages, and besides giving me excellent fare they provided much useful information. Their cottage adjacent to the road had been built near a twisting market beasts' track, being straightened recently as mechanized road-making has been introduced. The Connell Ballachulish Railway closed these few years has meant greatly increased road transport, the little old port jetty piles rotting in disuse.

Their house still on the old plan, built ages ago, consists of huge corner quoins, the main stones being built head on into the fiercest winds. These were hauled or dragged on sleds or sledges and levered up ramps of earth to their positions. Roofs to such properties in old times consisted of tree timbers untrimmed, with coverings of rushes, sods and mud with a stolid chimney—part of a gable—reeking out blue peat smoke.

In the area are a number of cottages whose origin would date back from Culloden, 1746, when returning soldiers were rewarded for services rendered to the Camerons by being allotted a portion of land each on which to build a one-roomed cottage, with the proviso the land would never be his. Even today, leases of crofts and cottages stipulate that such be handed down from father to son, and should the family discontinue, any would-be tenant applications must be made through the Land and the Crofters' Commissions, providing a healthy conservation to keep Scotland for the Highlanders.

There is a magnificent vista from Mr and Mrs Shaw's cottage and plot of land which reaches to the water's edge, overlooking Loch Linnhe to the mountains of Ardnamurchan, and on this and neighbours' land are as yet unearthed barrows which would reveal sacred remains of revered people of past ages. In olden times the bodies of deceased nobles would be brought overland to this region with the cortège halting for the night before being ferried to the burial isle of Iona.

This same area was chosen by Robert Louis Stevenson for *Kidnapped*, for overpowering mountain heights, wooded ravines and torrents abound—grand escape ground for fugitives. The author must have seen a memorial to 'Red Fox' a laird's factor, who was shot in the back while collecting rents from an Argyll village and making his way through the woods for further collections. However, instead of the real villain being punished, a James Stewart was convicted and hung from a gibbet, whose poor relatives were forbidden to remove his body until the carrion crows had devoured all flesh from his skeleton.

Not far on the wild road to Crianlarich one passes through notorious Glen Coe; and even yet, since that dastardly massacre of thirty-eight people on a February day in 1692, a sense of hostility exists between the two clans concerned, namely, Macdonalds and Campbells. Out in the Hebrides, I personally addressed a man in error as Mr Campbell, who strongly emphasized the denial of such a name, so the feeling pitiably is still widespread. It is to be hoped these two fine communities will, concerning themselves, 'bury the hatchet', for on my journey I used both clan members for my hospitality and found them equally excellent.

Round Ballachulish at one time men's lives were forfeit for poaching to satisfy the hunger of their starving families. Like starlings which always have a lookout, these dour men would trap deer, hares, or even rabbits and carry them home in the darkness, having the carcases shared and in the pot with all traces of hides buried, for the men to avoid confrontation.

Mr Shaw, a retired naval superior, spoke on the casual attitude to sailing many inexperienced people exhibit as they negotiate the treacherous narrow strait which admits and empties tides from Loch Leven. Near the ferry, Peter's stone is a reminder of the drowning of a Viking leader who perished trying to free a foundered vessel from the shore. It is fascinating to watch the swirling eddies caused by strong tides with a following wind, but deadly for those inexperienced, underestimating their power.

I had wondered where I would sleep, when Mrs Shaw hoisted a map-pole to a ring in the ceiling, and pulled down a trap door, revealing a steep ladder to two bedrooms in the underdrawn rafters. The way she brought morning coffee for me up the ladder at her age is a miracle, and soon I descended from the 'heavenly' regions to prepare for my journey.

Outside a fearful wind had developed, and I was strongly dissuaded from setting out. A near hurricane roared between Beinn-a-Bheithir on the Argyll side and two mountains on the northern flanks of the loch, yet I felt in October fiercer gales might blow and prepared to leave. I 'battened down', and hoisted my bag filled with a feast of delights crammed in furtively by Mrs Shaw, and said "Goodbye". How I stood on that elevated road, let alone walked, was amazing. I grasped the hedge and struggled to the ferry-landing. No wonder the ferry wasn't running. The water was 'mad', and waves washing up the slipway revealed I would have to go some twenty miles round to get to the other side, a mere quarter mile.

"Fair's fair!" A motorist forlornly waiting for me to report findings gladly conveyed me to Glencoe and then I walked three extra miles to offset that little distance that could not be crossed. Nowhere else did I resort to any lift, only ferry landing to ferry landing.

I have never seen more leaden skies in my life as on this, my worst morning. The wind, like a tornado, tore on through the gully from Glen Coe and forced me to take to the old railway track to get shelter from the alders, and ironically as I reached the ferry it had begun, in still stormy conditions.

Continuing on this grim occasion, a youth must have been surprised to see anyone about. We chatted a moment, when the door of his home opened, his mother telling me to come and share Sunday dinner with them. Mrs Ritchie's kindness and the goodwill of her husband and family brightened that day, as I paced tenaciously that dreary track which formerly was the most glorious railway known to me.

Kent Allen and Duror slipped by, on a good day places which beggar description, but now only the hint of the sky's sullenness showed, as spaces appeared between flotillas of inky-black clouds which gave no opportunity for photography.

Six miles yet it was to Appin, on a day of silence, where began the most memorable journey of my life, as the shore of Loch Linnhe revealed the mysterious sheen of evening on the vast stretch of water, separating the peninsula from the mainland. Dark clouds sailed in a sea of turquoise and crimson, as the dying sun, hidden all day, shed an aura like the glow of Vesuvius over the distant Mountains of Mull.

An unmistakable presence of God flooded my being in this vast landscape when the thought recurred, "The earth is the Lord's and the fulness thereof", for every stride brought fresh wonders. At last the sleeping village of Appin showed its welcome, as a crescent moon shone over the bay where Castle Stalker stood sentinel, and cows coughed to show their awareness as I took a time exposure from the steep field, and then found accommodation.

19 *Authors, Witches, Poets and A' That*

STALKER Castle there in the shallows, once the hunting seat of James IV, serene and benign like a King Canute, appeared to watch my steady recession from this region of mysterious and mountainous land, the very spot for hiding miscreants or refugees.

The landscape changed into delta areas of good land and lowland farms, with a factory for ice-cream and jelly making, since seaweed, a necessary product in manufacturing, is so readily available round about. "Hello, Hello, what are you up to?" might have asked the retired police sergeant as he inquisitively enquired of my project. "You haven't seen better chrysanthemums than these anywhere, have you?" I told him a fib, it would have been unfair to start Sergeant Macalpine's blood pressure rising: "Yes, aren't they beauties?"

"Och aye," he added proudly, and let me go.

The hot, blistering road was terrible to walk upon and any and everything encouraged me to halt: blackberries, foliage, and an old cottage; I had gained four miles by 'cheating' in trespassing over the old Loch Creran railway bridge, thus saving a huge detour. Eventually I came across a fine, clean stretch of road which is maintained litter-free by Oban schoolchildren—a great credit to them and well worthy of emulation by other young people.

I had made this journey on many previous occasions, but now it was agony for every step, yet in spite of this I recall the glorious aspects of Mull, Lismore, and Kingairloch across the glistening Firth of Lorn; and landwards the magnificent overpowering mass of Ben Cruachan (3689 feet), triumphant in the electric blue of a sharp sky, seemed to dominate that supremest of waters, Loch Etive.

To anyone staying in the vicinity of Oban, this is a 'must' in any itinerary, to sail up Loch Etive its full length of eighteen miles, completely shut off from mankind, and see the wildest of mountains about which, with some fortune, eagles and stags may be seen.

I had done a fair day's tramp and stood like a Goliath amongst the ironwork of Connel Ferry Bridge looking down at the fierce whirlpools, as the ebb tide eddying, emptied over the falls of Lora towards the sea. It paralysed my thinking to see down from this great height and made me fear for the nerves of men who made the scaffolding to make the bridge.

This massive structure built in 1903 saves a huge detour in northerly directions of four times the length of the journey to Fort William and avoids travelling over a wilderness of moorland. It stands with two main features—grappling cantilevers similar in design to the Old Forth Bridge, which seem like two wrestling contestants in a deathly combat.

Old Mr Mackinson, seventy-five, excitedly told me how he had seen it opened to rail, then road and rail traffic, and so recently in 1966 again only used for road vehicles and pedestrians. He regretted the changing times which has caused the loss of sixteen men's work, as now only one man is used on the station. Finding accommodation, I was glad to ease my *dreadful feet* before hobbling towards the hospitable Dunstaffnage Arms, for a splendid meal—'on the management'.

Next, using sponge-rubber pads shaped to ease my sores, I forged on through great trees to Taynuilt. For myself, I wish oases of timber-free places were available, they would give occasional sights of watery expanses. A layby at intervals would give pleasure to many, avoiding monotony of the sameness of too much of a good thing.

However, I stopped as two lorrymen, glad to have a word, told me of one Duke of Argyll, who received a demand note from the King of England to hand over Rob Roy Macgregor, as he was stealing cattle from over the border. The duke replied, "If I am sheltering him and your majesty is feeding him, we'll call it quits."

I was told Taynuilt was the former rail terminus before

Oban was reached, thus becoming the capital of the west. Hitherto a former road mender, Mr Macnicol told me his job had been to maintain the old coach road by keeping the highway free from pools and ruts. He would dig out trouble spots and put in a hard core of large stones, then some boulder clay and finally small stones on top. It used to be a backaching job, smashing down large stones for the top coverings, using a small-headed hammer with a pliant hazel-twig shaft to avoid hand blisters. He would not allow me to leave without proudly showing me his tidy stone-built shed, which still possessed the ancient roof with a sturdy wooden roof truss fastened together by wooden pins to save the use of iron straps and bolts. The pins still projected either side, one-time pegs on which to hang horse harness.

It was lunch hour for the shop-keeper, but no trouble for her as she came willingly to serve me and told me about her village. Goodwill always extended to the English, since even before the Napoleonic War, English craftsmen brought trade into the village by smelting iron from the supplies of bog iron, for copious supplies of timber for charcoal, making furnace fuel, was available in the area. These 'foreigners' behaved well and were equally well received, in fact the first British statue to Nelson was erected in the locality.

As I finished the diversion round the village, I heard joiners working and looked in another tidy workplace where Robert Macnicol and his young assistant were busy. "Have you anything you would care to show me you have made?" I asked.

"Yes, Mister. When you pass through Loch Awe village, just look in St Conan's church at the altar table I assisted in making when I was a young man!"

On the main road the overpowering mass of Ben Cruachan glowered down almost denying room for road and rail alongside another magnificent loch, Loch Awe. In order to make a wider road, even as I passed tremendous queues of vehicles were waiting until a huge crane had manipulated a giant cantilever in position upon stalwart stanchions deep in the water.

Every time I pass this gloomy area with the opposite shore screes, and the towering Cruachan's threatening height, I unfailingly think Awe is the name, and awful the scene! On

Castle Maol, Kyleakin, Isle of Skye, on a rainy Sunday morning

A view from the ferry landing at Kyleakin

At Elgol on the Isle of Skye; the Cuillins are behind the pall of cloud

My best photograph, taken from a boat while crossing the Sound of Sleat

Evening in Mallaig

The 'first and last rocks' (which I passed in darkness). Loch-nan-Uamh, near where Bonnie Prince Charles left Britain for ever

Appin Castle by moonlight. (Notice the head of the inquisitive cow on the left, which indirectly caused movement of the camera.) For the photographically minded, the exposure was 20 seconds at f3.5.

I waded to get this shot of Kilchurn Castle on Loch Awe

Inveraray Castle and bridge

A Loch Eck farm. Just before this photograph was taken, a stag roared his challenge from the heights

Loch Eck

Sanquhar Post Office

Above: By the shore of Ullswater, near Patterdale. A huge bull was loose near me when I took this shot. *Below:* Old Fred the cowman at Plumpton on the former Roman road near Penrith. (The Council issued the red flag – before the motorway came, this was Britain's most dangerous road.)

a grim day in unenlightened times, one could well imagine giants hurling javelins of fire in a thunderstorm. Even today in the security of a railway carriage the threshing engine can be heard assailing the track to Glen Lochy and the outside world.

I reached the renowned Cruachan Hydro-Electric Scheme offices and went to ask for information about this exciting application of man's ingenuity. The offices were closing when a fellow Yorkshireman heard my voice. "Want to look round?"

"Please, but I must press on to find digs," I said.

"I'll fix that from 'underneath'," he replied, and soon we were whisked away in a van three-quarters of a mile into the mountain. From the office in that Aladdin's cave, he phoned for my accommodation and then showed me the huge turbines which are operated by the flow of water through giant pipes leading from a reservoir 1300 feet higher on the mountain.

He explained that during peak periods, current is generated for the grid system, but when the load is lessened, where such systems as atomic power stations must by their nature keep producing, some of this off-peak current is used to pump back water from Loch Awe into the manmade reservoir to provide maximum load power next day. To illustrate this splendid system, alongside this monster hall, bigger than many public places, a large mural depicts a fable about the past ages when it was believed a witch lived on the mountain. She supposedly controlled the springs and streams which were allowed to flow in the daytime, but while men slept remained awake to staunch the water supply. In weariness one night she slept, failing to stop the waters, which flooded the land, becoming Loch Awe, a huge fifteen square miles' lake, which drowned all the people. As if to make amends, some clever 'wizards' have set into operation this wonderful scheme which has brought work to the people locally and provided benefits nationally.

Och aye, my digs B. Airton 'fixed' were splendid; but from a technical angle this thrill afforded me by Mr Airton and his superior Mr Craven was my best on route and not to be missed by tourists.

Before setting off on this 'sticky' morning, I visited St

Conan's church, an unusual structure making much use of daylight, when I noticed Robert Macnicol's work on the altar table; it justified his pride. Closing the door, my journey into the outer world seemed one of sorrow and weeping. Trees forlornly hung their branches with leaves drenched with fine rain, and familiar mountains lost their defiant splendour in a heavy pall of mist. The beautiful ruin of Kilchurn Castle, one so frequently used as a superb subject for artists and photographers, could scarce be seen. I left the scene of dejection, the ruin guarding the loch in awe, whilst the Highland cattle squelched through muddy tracks looking through shaggy, drenched hair for any grassy morsels overlooked by others. Once a Scotch cow lowered her horns in defence of her young calf as I approached incautiously, but no hostility was shown today as we shared these melancholy conditions.

I could have ruminated on Omar Khayyám, "Oh what a sorry state is this," but looked for the beauty of wetness along the wild moorland road of Glen Aray, where shrouded mountains and racing torrents, domain of the wild stag and his hinds, of cattle and sheep and carrion crows, seemed as it had ever been; as for myself, I was Alexander Selkirk—'monarch of all I surveyed'.

Sheer resolution took me first past the halted army vehicle and its morose driver, whose contingent had gone searching the wilderness for an unexploded bomb dropped on a wartime bombing zone; and then the cottage half hidden in brushwood where 'William' sat amongst his collection of old books. He looked miserable as did his dog—a good meal would have done both good, yet he insisted on giving me a coffee. He badly needed companionship: "Give me a nice wife and a family, and I'd be a happy man," he said as we shook hands.

Soon the high ramparts of Inveraray showed in the dispersing clouds, the high lookout hill of over 1000 feet showing its advantageous siting for observation of the glen approaches, which must have saved the fine old town from many intruders in past days.

No exception to my visitation took place, for Mrs Ramsay at the youth hostel very kindly gave me an excellent meal, and fine hospitality—I needed it after such a 'sticky' journey.

20 *Bonnie Argyll*

ARCHITECTURALLY Inveraray seems like a jewelled brooch; it is only a small town with a gorgeous setting on Loch Fyne, and sparkles with fine old shops with a modern approach. The ferry across to St Catherines has ceased and the old pier supports a lamp post no longer used. One hot day, watching millions of fry plying about the pier's timbers, shining like platinum as they changed course, I said "I wouldn't mind a swim, Frank Hepworth," when a chorus of boys yelled "There's a shark!" a remark verified by some adults. That cooled my ardour, a basking shark, though said to be harmless.

The town is maintained by the National Trust, for such jewels as the Old Arch, and the Bell Tower with its fine carillon, must be preserved at all costs. Then the old church divided in two for Gaelic and English services is beautiful and the famous road bridge by the castle is superb with its 'turned' newels and fine arches. Further, Neil Munro the poet's dwelling, amongst the old salt houses with their iron balustrades and steps to higher floors, intrigued me. I was shown inside one house to see the brick arched ceiling, for the floors supporting such heavy loads of salt could not be made of wood as decaying timber from the 'sweat' would have been dangerous.

Having photographed old Alexander Graham's small iron field plough, a product of his hobby, from the larger work of his trade of blacksmithing, I set off into one of the wettest regions of Britain on a pleasant morning.

Tantalizingly St Catherines was not more than 1½ miles across the Loch but it would take me a day's march to reach it. The sight of the white cottages and town buildings of Inveraray together with beautiful headlands and reaches of glimmering water was superb; yet as I passed the old Dunderage Castle (Doom) there seemed to be a hint of change as a grey pall drifted over the headlands.

A sombre strath and pasturage revealed some farms and the bungalow of one Archibald Callander, a bachelor, who is a light engineer, and very modern, for he uses a very large, completely flat bench upon which he makes farm gates for stock and to order, using bottled gas for welding purposes. On some projects too large to handle himself, with the aid of his mother and lever manipulation they manipulate the work to facilitate his drilling and riveting, and so his workshop is full of contentment. Archie wouldn't let me pass until after a tea break, when having looked at his prize begonias and geraniums, I entered the 'monsoon region'.

To the accompaniment of steady rain, I went into Cairndow post office, replete with kindness, and saw a middle-aged woman veteran cyclist quietly set off pedalling into the downpour with four large deer hounds trotting either side of her machine. They encouraged me to leave the cheery shop to next assail Kilmorich church called the round church, so built that the Devil could not find a corner to hide in.

Used for TV productions of *Dr Finlay's Casebook*, this beautiful building had no 'following' on this grim day; however I could not usher out one visitor, a trapped sparrow, and thinking to avoid it injury, I went and told the folk living close by to deal with it.

The Devil could find no room inside, but by Jove, he had prepared for me outside as I forged up the hill into Glen Kinglas with high mountains about, in intense gloom. The rain was torrential and when at last the great detour gave direction past Hell's Glen down the dark road, I hacked at the rain belt notch after notch, making the miles tick by, until the little lights twinkled in the houses of St Catherines. I had found myself in the complete loneliness, singing—what else but Sir Harry Lauder's 'Keep right on to the——end'!

It was exasperating to sit at breakfast and positively see vehicles entering Inveraray so near, and yet it had taken me a soaking to get to St Catherines.

Again foot blisters dreadfully painful had developed by getting wet feet and yet I had to turn out, and pressed on an unfortunate mileage where trees blotted out the view of the water. (I repeat, if only a few spaces were allowed, the serious rambler could get away from the road and see some fine scenery unhampered.) Eventually Strachur stretched along an open shore, a fine little place, with cottage walls and gardens competing in the splendour of flowers; and sternly watched from a little park by a fine mansion—a typically Scotch residence—of Sir Fitzroy Maclean, M.P., the author of *A Concise History of Scotland*.

Turning south-east towards Dunoon, I seemed to be in Austria, with the noise of saws on the mountains and the rising plumes of blue wood smoke from the busy sawmill drifting up the 2000-foot slopes. The keen tang of smoke was replaced by the aroma of pines in the huge forest, which opened on to the estate of the late Sir Harry Lauder; and far down the narrow valley the long 'eel' of water, Loch Eck, stretched peacefully with an angler's boat drifting gently as evening closed in.

At the first house near the road, I asked about lodgings when Kenneth Johnson's wife put the kettle on, whilst the tough, curly-headed 33-year-old woodsman told me of his proud independence. He buys areas of timber—though not the land—and fells the trees, selling logging material to Strachur Mill and smaller logs for pallet-making to Workington in Cumberland. He uses the best forestry equipment from Norway and employs extra help when required. As a family of four they are proud to own their own house, and though remote from a sizeable village, yet the children get to a good school by using the school's transport system.

Loch Eck is different from the 'open' highland waters, for it is flanked by tremendous pine-covered slopes, yet it offers more to the naturalist where hides can be readily camouflaged. Well might a Thoreau build his cabin thereabouts, and live in bliss undisturbed for ever. A pair of swans drifted by, half hidden by lochside alders, as I looked for the village of Whistlefield to get my digs.

A wagtail perched on the boat end of the inn sign as I looked for the elusive place, but having passed a handful of dwellings, I asked a farmer returning home where I could stay. "With me," Ian Grant replied.

The young farmer and his wife fêted me well, and as he had chores to do after my meal, he hurried in to me from the yard saying, "Quick, listen!" We rushed out, held our breaths, and high from the 2000-foot mountains we heard the roars and echoes of challenging stags.

Their farm house at the foot of Beinn Ruadh with its lighted windows looked like a phantom palace, which prompted me to take a photograph.

"Lend me some steps, please."

"What for?"

I told him why.

"Och, ye can't at this time o'night," he said in disbelief, yet some months later he was surprised with the result. The rest of the night he told me they tenant a 22-acre farm which supports two cows and four calves; and if a good growing season is apparent, he buys and rears six bullocks for the October sales. General farming is impossible since rainfalls come at the wrong time, so grass is encouraged by lime, slag and manure.

To maintain a livelihood he does extraneous work like wood-cutting, fencing, and deer-stalking; and fishing, "to keep sane". The two of them, with an ageing aunt, also provide 'bed and breakfast' and run boarding kennels. For relaxation they attend *Ceilidhs*, a Gaelic form of concert-cum-dance, and 'run down' to Dunoon for shopping.

"When there's a strike, and you're without food and fuel, come a 'million strides' back and stay with us at Island Farm, we've plenty of each to spare," he said.

One old lady nearby dreads this infernal age of modernism, for she says, "Folk were a lot healthier before 'they' invented these damn vitamins," and what's worse, is "this sudden death"—a dreadful thing—"it would kill a horse"!

Our mutual exchanges done, I was able to phone home from the very house where I was staying, telling of the great attention I was getting; and soon up and off, I felt a certain nostalgia in leaving Scotland's great pride—the mountains! A dull morning with a great pall of mist over the loch and into the mountain gullys provided the most wonderful aerial display of my life, as a powerful sun crept over the summits dispersing in awesome movements the magic white veil, to reveal the wonderful autumn colours of trees. Reaching Ben More Gardens, huge sequoias line the paths through this spectacular arboretum until a fantastic view leads the eye into the great glen with its receding mountain ridges. Hereabouts are Britain's highest trees in this warm, moist climate; and as one looks from the lily pond, a sense that nature's showpiece is situated in reasonable reach of Glasgow's population who want a good day's outing.

The gardens left behind, the delta lands at the fet of great glens spread out in rich pasturage of fields, bordered with modern sporadic building, and naval vessels; and fitting out ships strangely filled the hazy backcloth to where American ratings seemed like busy ants moving to and fro on busy missions. I was at Holy Loch and 'civilization', and quickly passed through to pleasant, busy Dunoon and the waiting ferry to Gourock.

A homesick naval rating sat opposite me as we quietly slipped across the placid Clyde with its draught-board shoulder gun emplacements at Cloch Point 'surveying' our progress. Backwards we were leaving the huge purple fingers of mountains between the silver lochs shimmering in the dipping sun. His eyes were vacant—his heart 3000 miles west —and mine ... When I crossed the road in Gourock, it was three hundred miles north until two young folk shouted as they raced towards me: "*Mr Kyme! Mr Kyme!* Hello there! How wonderful you look!"

"Sorry my dears, I don't know you."

"We saw you at Kylesku, do you remember?"

"Of course, young friends, you were dressed differently then—my heart's still up there, shall we go back?"

I shall never forget trying to get accommodation until when quite dark at the 'draught board', where many docile caravans looked across the inky Clyde, one opened its door and gave me a splendid welcome into the Sheriffs of Glasgow's already crowded holiday home.

21 *Into Burns Country*

To avoid using the Glasgow–Gretna A74 busy road, I decided to follow the coast to Ayr, but required no alarm clock to awaken me to the task. The heat of the previous sunny day and the cool of evening caused a dense fog over all the area, and since the caravan was situated within a stone's throw of Cloch Point lighthouse, the *Ooooumph* of the fog horn made sleep impossible. It was fascinating for all that, for after each call of the horn, a strong echo came nine seconds afterwards, and yet a fainter one at eleven seconds, reflected from the mountains over the water; these echoes were indicative of the terrific initial boom. Breakfast over, the Sheriffs and their dog after being so kindly tolerant after all the upheaval of fitting me into their small confines, saw me off in fine style towards Largs.

There's nothing astir in Scotland on a Sunday morning except worshippers, and maybe a few energetic cyclists who relish the idea of traffic-free roads. I was off at a cracking pace when a cyclist insisted on tracking me from the comforts of his saddle. It was most enjoyable to have a companion for a few miles, since the fog withheld the beautiful scenery of the nearby Clyde.

To Largs only was a short day, so hearing a church bell I went into a back pew and enjoyed myself at little Inverkip, where in spite of my walking gear, the elders of the church seemed delighted for me to share in their service.

It was very soon, the sun having lifted the fog, that an intense drowsiness overtook me at Wemyss Bay, whereupon I copied a few others, except that I had the good fortune of a rucksack pillow and dozed off. Three-quarters of an hour slipped by, when the shrill laughter of playing children brought me to reality, and I set off again.

It was amazing the difference of the period up to noon as

compared with afternoon; it happened to be Bank Holiday when all the folk of Scotland who possessed cars seemed to be out on a tour through Glasgow to Ayr and back. A vehicle every one or two seconds passed by, until I reached Largs, where I was glad to call it a day.

Largs was chill next morning, but that was more than offset by its courteous people who were so helpful I would be induced to go and holiday there. It is a charming little place sheltered from the east and renowned for sunsets settling over the Isle of Bute. Furthermore it is a centre for touring both to attractive coastal resorts or easily arranged sea trips to delightful islands. I called for mail at the 'closed' post office, and by being helped by the staff who didn't mind a Sassenach calling, received what was due to me and then turned towards 'Heaven'—at least that's what everyone called it when I asked for Irvine.

Fairlie, a beautiful little spot even on this grim, windy day, has a threat of an impending steel works project taking over some of this delectable area. "Ah well, work will be found for the local people," versus "These money-grabbers will take every acre of ground worth seeing away from us for ever." I sympathized with the man who had bought his house near the shore—an old house—that had seen family after family enjoying the sights and sounds of the sea. He will be offered ready cash, heaps of it, to lose his claim on that blessed plot; but where else will money purchase such a haven any more? They are all fast disappearing.

Grinding off the miles from Stevenston to Irvine, I was to see how a difficult problem is solved at Seamill Post Office, for on a beautifully script-written card easily to be seen was the canny message, "We are particular about the cleanliness of this shop as you are of your home. Will you kindly explain this to your dog?"

On I went past some miles of boulder-strewn shore with strips of sand enough to carefully canter along on horseback, when a long patch of grass appeared like a Cambridge college lawn, adjoining it being the tidiest farm I had yet seen. Though the weather was rough and dull, an old man was using side-cutting shears to keep the verges neat. He stopped, seeing me, referring to me as 'young man', revealing he was eighty-seven, and the self-imposed task found him something to do. We parted, John Kean and I, and as I walked towards Stevenston I felt he ought to be chairman for a Tidier Britain Committee—he would get things moving, if even by example alone.

The shore seemed to finish squarely, terminated by some large, modern works; I thereby had to strike into the Stevenston township avoiding the coast. I was informed how these modern industries of the coastal towns are contributing in a large way to boosting export trading, even entering the Japanese market with sporting equipment.

I pressed on to reach Irvine before dark; it was not to be, however, since old Jimmy Sinclair, the retired poet-plasterer, when I answered his salutation, invited me home to have tea, and pressed. I yielded ultimately to accept a Scots bow-tie to wear.

I was soon out of the town into the open, threshing on to Irvine tramping alongside a modern road which seemed to be the new order right down even to Ayr which I followed the next day. For company much of the time was the great roar of airliners entering or leaving Prestwick Airport. Incidental to this, but nevertheless important, was the system of loud shots and flares for scaring the birds from the vicinity of the runways, so with one noise and another, not least the traffic, I reached the outskirts of Ayr and snoozed off by the side of the river.

Aroused, I walked by the riverside past a delightful mansion called Craigie House, then forward into the town. Even in twilight the shore was attractive with its memories of Burns, who must have watched so often the setting sun over Arran before turning home to Alloway. It is only a few miles along the shore at Culzean Castle where General Eisenhower made his residence during part of the wartime; and in the town itself John Knox preached in the now ruined church. The Wallace Tower looked grim in the fading light and added character to the skyline of buildings, while cranes with their lighted jibs moved silently across the little harbour where last fishing boats raced in before dark. The 'season' had finished, and now as I left the edge of the dark, lapping water and strolled alongside the solemn parade of promenade railings, I saw no one, and went in to make my log.

I left Ayr the pleasant holiday centre and struck out eastwards to Cumnock, not without some misgivings, for I was leaving the sea, that element which always holds me in a hypnotic spell. I thought as I wandered:

> There is nought on Earth just like the sea.
> That calm or rough, or blue or grey,
> I'd like to walk by every day
> To follow the tide and feel the spray,
> That is the life, to be free, ere free.

It was better to be on a country road again with the natural hedgerows instead of thousands of posts, railings, and concrete bridges.

The hedges interspersed with a few trees indicated the prevailing winds from the coast, all the trunks inclining by at least fifteen degrees to the leeward side and some specimens of hardwood trees had not one branch growing to the windward. It is an ill wind that blows no one good, and particularly this morning I was helped on splendidly. It seemed like England once again since large bushes sheltered the highway and leafy canopies hung overhead. I had noticed that Scotland seems to be divided into three sections: one down to Gairloch, Ross-shire, with no fences by roadsides, Gairloch to the Clyde with wooden posts and wire fencing, and Ayr to Gretna—fences interspersed with pleasant hedgerows and roadside trees, or forestry plantations.

I enjoyed this freedom from traffic and was able to concentrate upon the gently undulating rural scene of huge farmlands; for now the deep browns of the Ordnance Survey map had yielded to pale yellow and even greens. This indicated, as it appeared, undramatic country but pleasant and restful to the eye. I had reached a farmstead called Carbeiston Byres—not quite really—but I did reach it with more determination than as yet in 300 miles. I was passing a weak-looking nominal fence with a cow not twenty yards away, with a large Friesian ringed bull not more than five yards from the fence. He obviously ignored traffic but could not have been familiar with pedestrians, for his large, staring eyes must have seen *red*, as I had plenty about me, when he let out the most fearsome roar, repeated, and yet again, with his brutish head lowered and all his interest removed from his courtship to my dismissal. I'm convinced if I'd stayed he would have killed me—I sadly wanted a photograph of this majestic beast, but his savage disapproval suggested discretion is the better part of valour. I moved on.

Occasionally the far vista would be lightened by a fitful sun, and rooftops of farmsteads miles away would glisten like burnished platinum after the intermittent showers. Mixed farming revealed the gathered crops and aftermath of stubble, while cows and sheep munched contentedly in security of pasturage, not like their kinds in the mountainous north which have to forage from the sparse ground in sometimes savage weather. I counted forty-seven beast in one field, indicative both of the lush yield of the ground and the size of herds and fields, yet strangely I had contemplated a landscape like to the coalfields of South Yorkshire grim and dirty. It was not so.

Meanwhile, Frank Gordon, a travelling salesman whose wares quenched my thirst, had contacted some press reporters who interviewed me as I walked, before finally reaching the town of Cumnock. I stayed the night in accommodation most courteously found me by helpful folk, and heard of their proud historical background of the Covenanters who wished to worship in their own chosen way, in spite of hostile opposition and eventual persecution.

Being a mining area, the inventive mind of William Murdock devised the making and using of coal gas, and also the gas mantle, thus warming and lighting homes and factories, which have proved a great asset to us since coal is an indigenous fuel.

They proudly speak of the cloth-capped politician Keir Hardie who, because of his declared principles, was 'blacked' from the mining industry by colliery owners, yet still represented his former workmates by pen and speech, until at last he could more forcibly represent them in parliament.

I had seen a curious phenomenon as I approached the town. Seeing a fellow over a neat stone wall, I clambered a grassy bank to note his activities when he told me the reason for some neatly stacked portions of gravestones set at the heads of many graves. He said that only a few years ago during the Glasgow gale, many stones were blown down and broken, but the ones still intact were all of granite. In spite of the broken piles of debris he had the tidiest cemetery I had ever seen, a great credit to him. However, I remarked, "Surely this rather small graveyard does not keep you in full-time occupation?" He replied, he attended to five such, and a colleague also had five in other distant villages. With a glint in his eye he told me that a visitor to his friend's area had given compliments, and added, "Mister, surely people don't die often in this lovely neighbourhood, do they?" "No, only once," he said.

A grim tale many still recall happened just along my way, at New Cumnock, some years ago, when colliers were working so near to the surface that water, which had accumulated in pools in wet weather, suddenly cascaded into the workings and drowned the unfortunate men without warning.

I was now in the rolling hill country so beloved by Burns, for here was the river which inspired his poem 'Afton Water'; I hope he saw it on a better day than this, for even the main-line railway looked listless as a lone seagull languidly glided down to an empty platform. The dull, grim weather afforded me a break from the monotony of plodding on, to having a word with the blacksmith, but there was no reeking yellow smoke from the hot shoe fitting to a horse's hoof, no clang of rhythmic hammering, but a painstaking care of the finer craft of making door-knockers. He said a doctor wishing to have a knocker symbolic of his profession of the apothecary asked the farrier if he could make one, so he designed a serpent, and made a chisel shaped to give a pattern for the scales. So successful was his venture that he is still making door-knockers for professional people and others also.

Continuing into the wide valley I wondered, "What do folk do out here besides farming?", when I noticed some mounds of earth with barricades at one side only—an arsenal of some kind I guessed. It was a firework factory, in a sensible place away from great danger risks.

Here the friendly lights of Sanquhar welcomed me to the town renowned for good manners, which I proved, for a fellow went right out of his way to take me where I wished to go. They were all the same; there is no wonder goodwill issues from the place as it has done for ages, for it is at Sanquhar where Britain had its first post office.

But something I shall always remember about Sanquhar is that on phoning home, my wife said she and Andrew and my dog Robbie would meet me next day. Would I tell them where I would be approximately at such a time? Excited is an overwrought word, but even so I slept well, and was soon away from the pleasant place next morning, passing the old ruined castle and leaving its people to making fireworks and knitted gloves.

In the open again the hills began to close in upon the valley so steeply that cultivation with machinery was impossible, in fact the roadside to the north bore up with terrific steepness to the highest village in Scotland at Wanlockhead, where gold was found and used for the royal jewellery. It seemed to me in this hill country as if the land were reverting back to Highland terrain, wild and hummocky to over 2000 feet. However, afforestation on lower slopes is getting afoot, and the wilder stretches being used for grouse moors and deer.

As I continued, that longed-for reunion soon happened when the car came round a bend with my wife and son, and it would be quite impossible to forget such moments when my dog realized at long last they had found his master.

It was at this happy time a fellow with a gun and a cycle smilingly came forward, for he seemed, as well he might at this strange reunion, a little bewildered. We explained the reason for the large rucksack and red stockings, and then he told us of his mission in the area. However, time was only too short before my folk had to be off, to wind up the day's journey of 500 miles to see me. They were soon gone ...

Robert Stewart, the stocky 47-year-old gamekeeper, reared up his gun and cycle against a tree, and revealed to me the interesting things concerning himself and the neighbourhood. He wore a large sports coat with good pockets, flannels tucked inside wellingtons, turned over at the tops to avoid irritation on his knees when cycling, a clean white shirt, collar and tie, deerstalker hat and large haversack. How do I know all this? I took his photograph, the best portrait of my whole journey *but*, he blinked in the 1/100-second of my shot or else you'd have seen it in the book. He had, as a boy, had game-keeping lessons from his father (also a keeper) and been in the service of the Duke of Buccleuch for twenty years. Along with other men he is involved in keeping the 160,000-acre estate in good order, for there is always a fair amount of vermin preying on birds and animals.

Since there is no fox hunting, such predators prey upon the game, and would continue to cause havoc unless dealt with in a humane way. Farmers also are glad to be rid of the foxes which in a locality breed from twenty to thirty litters of cubs with probably seven cubs to each litter. The cubs are born from mid-April onwards in earths that are usually in the same area every year. To be rid of the animals, terriers are used to bolt them from the earths and then they are shot.

Hooded crows are a menace to game also, and will clean out a nest of partridge or pheasant eggs in a matter of hours. To rid the area of these birds requires strategy from the keepers, and the cunning method used to lure the birds towards a gun is, to lay a 'trap' of hens' eggs—which they enjoy. Before the eggs are placed, a hide is built with branches and bracken and the trap then laid. These birds are poor counters, and are outwitted from their place of observation when two keepers go to the hide and one leaves, the crow believing the hide to be empty goes to the nest, and is of course shot.

"Well, what about your appetite after being out in the open on the tops of Wanlockhead all those miles from Thornhill?"

"You ask my wife who looks after me well, what I like after a cold day. She provides tatties and mince, or Scotch broth; and as a sweet a clootie dumpling." (A clootie is a cloth wrapped around some dried fruit, spices, flour, sugar and milk, which have been kneaded together into a large ball, and then boiled. For birthdays, they are made extra large, replete with coins as surprises, and what is left over is sliced and eaten cold, or fried.)

Pulling his leg, I said, "Now Mr Stewart, what about a change occasionally, say a nice roasted cock pheasant, that would be a home-coming, a nice change of diet?" However, he made a 'diversion' to the Drumlanrig Castle, one of the largest in the south of Scotland to which the Duke and Duchess of Buccleuch invite the Royal Family; it is so palatial that there are as many windows as days in a year, and rooms as weeks in a year also, therefore there is much work required in managing such a mansion and the huge estate, and if Robert Stewart were an example of the employees and personnel then they are a happy people.

The game-keeper mounted his cycle, gun and all, and I behind him more slowly followed on towards Thornhill and Auldgirth with the ultimate gloom of evening closing in.

There was a nostalgia as the throbbing diesel locos pulled in the little stations and tired workers tramped down the steep tracks to the roadway, when the locos would give their whooping coughs and pass out into the drear beyond with the remainder of Dumfries commuters.

Again on and on into the twilight and darkness, with here and there cottage lights gleaming until I reached another halting place that ended another good day's march: I had reached Auldgirth and stayed with Mrs Craig at the post office. After settling down, I asked for information about the past that had influence in the district and further afield, for I could tell of her ability immediately as she allowed me to read one of her prize-winning essays in competitions.

She said when she was a girl over sixty years ago, poverty was such as to limit footwear for winter use only, as in summer the bairns ran about barefooted. To help with washing blankets these were immersed in a large tub, and then she tramped them barefooted saving a back-breaking job for her mother.

The locality is, of course, rich in Burns lore for it is only two miles from Auldgirth at Ellisland Farm where he worked; and furthermore friars used to live in the area by reason of place names used, like Monks' Lodge and Friars' Carse, the flat stretches by the River Nith. Before setting off again I wandered about the Carse of the beautiful river—which flows on through Dumfries—and looked at the beautiful, massive stone bridge, for my father was a mason himself, whereas the mason for this bridge was the father of Thomas Carlisle. Thomas himself lived in the district for a while, until, becoming famous, he went to Chelsea.

The radio had indicated *rain*, so having made extra care nothing of importance would get wet, I left Auldgirth, determined to do as many miles as possible before the weather would limit progress. It proved one of my nicest days with lots of sunshine and only a few spots of drizzle.

Probably the proximity to Solway Firth provided suitable climate for the rich farming area I passed through, for the land which looked bountiful supported cattle and sheep, and the corn now harvested, giving an aftermath of glowing stubble like a Constable canvas, surrounded by sturdy deciduous trees now turned from summer's greens to the rich tones of later year. The hedgerows, some markedly thick hawthorn due to good layering, had the embellishment of topiary work examples showing badgers trotting along the tops. Eventually I came to a bungalow hedge with a similar animal atop, done so skilfully by a Mr Howie, but wonder ceased when I saw the village sign indicate I was in Hollywood. But, who knows who influences the other, for yet more badgers were about, some being done for a relaxation by a director of the Bank of England, a Mr Kissock.

At last I reached Dumfries, the Mecca of so many visitors to Scotland who sometimes put the poet before his country. I can in a measure agree with them, for when Scotland was to me only an area on a map of Britain, I had formulated a mental picture of a cottage interior and its inmates by reading and re-reading Burns's 'Cotter's Saturday Night'! My old headmaster too had thrilled me many times by his recitals of the poet's works, so that when I did see Dumfries, where Robert lived and died, it was with a real reverence I saw his statue outside Greyfriar's church.

Here I forgot the Saturday afternoon traffic, having running through my mind the inscriptions in the statue: "The rank is but the guineas's stamp", "The man's the Gowd for a' that", and left the clean town—home of the soccer team 'Queen of the South' which originally meant, and still does, the tidiest town you will find anywhere.

The open landscape soon appeared and keen air drifted in from the estuary giving a strong hint of wind to follow; and asking (after I'd done, by my reckoning, sixteen miles) if there were any likelihood of houses beyond Carrutherstown in my reach before night, I took the advice to stay in the local public house in the village.

22 *Across the Border*

It was with mixed feelings of regret and elation I set out from Carrutherstown on this last day of the marathon through Scotland into my own country. I had learned why Scots are so passionate in their love for their own land, and it would be mine by adoption if I didn't believe that the earth should be free for all. The wind, fierce from the Solway, savagely blew sideways on my striding, yet 3½ miles were 'clocked on' in the first hour. This was an inspiration, for I felt it would be possible to get well on the way to Carlisle by dark.

The hedgerows protecting me from the wind, and the healthy noisome manure odours from the farmlands, gave added impetus to my resolve, and soon the sea stretching down to the south-west came into view.

I posted a shoal of cards to well-wishers and leaving Gretna, looked at the desolate smithy now bereft of legality to unite runaway lovers, and crossed the border. There was a stroke of irony hereabouts, for I could not get a meal anywhere, so had to return again into Gretna; and by the time this was over it was soon dark.

Many times in my journeying did some individual enthusiasts retort "Oh I do wish I could come with you, I really do!" but if they had been on this long, windswept stretch of road into England on a dark night asking for accommodation, they would have relinquished the task.

Sleeping only fitfully, I made efforts to be off early after breakfast and was soon on the road, the new one, which speeds traffic to and from the border. To eyes and ears polite I would not offend by words of detail, but I reached Carlisle with only the will to hold on—thank goodness it was my last experience of dehydration. Calling at the first place that sold liquid, I had a 'pint' (you are wrong), a pint of milk. No better! Then turned into a café for a strong coffee, and another; I daren't ask for another, and wobbled on to another place and had orange juice, and two ripe bananas. "Ah, a bit better," and sauntered on through the Carlisle I'd seen before in better circumstances.

To steam loco enthusiasts, of course, this city is Mecca with the grand station and network of lines; and close by the soft glow of the red sandstone cathedral invited me in, but this day I was not in the mood for reverie and plodded on.

At last after another satisfying thirst quencher, my strength returned, and I gathered pace enough to satisfy and to astonish myself in completing nineteen miles in one day.

"But not so quickly! What did you see in the meantime?"

Much wasn't written about Carlisle, because everyone knows the city's connection with the Roman occupation. Even now excavations are contemplated for further 'finds', since evidence of a Roman brickworks has been found near Carleton.

Carlisle of course, by its position, is of great agricultural importance for mixed farming, even though not far away there are bleak fells and mountains. It was for a change a beautiful day and the road free of traffic like a country lane; yet at one time it was the busiest in all Britain with many serious and fatal accidents upon it. This beautiful road in its first uses would bear much droving whether legally or illegally; but before the new motorway began functioning, this Carlisle–Penrith stretch bore all the Scottish traffic. The fatalities were caused by the undulating surface which momentarily would hide vehicles overtaking from both directions when even careful drivers would be drawn into these 'death traps'. Now, as a result of experience, zigzag areas are marked on these sharp humps to prevent overtaking where one can't see far enough ahead.

It was sublime walking in a vast area where one could see all around for miles, with occasional stone-built farms with their alert off-duty dogs guarding their territories. Eventually my way led through the hamlet of Low Hesket which was asleep on the warm afternoon. If I had been there four months before there would have been bedlam with the traffic —now switched to the M6. I waited for someone to appear, when old Mr Duers told me that along my trail on the old Roman road, I would come to the top of a long rise where one could see for great distances from all points of the compass. At one time at this place a large thorn bush used to grow and there had always been such a bush as vouched for by local lore; it was here that annually the Thorn Parliament was held for all the huge district, where criminal cases and sheep-stealing offences would be tried. Also taxation for the area was levied by the appointed court; but on this day when I reached the place there was no toll or collector, so on I trekked and through High Hesket with its little church and outside belfry and mounting steps.

Periodically in neighbourly fashion a couple of farms would stand, with their shippons and barns, only shouting distance from each other to share facilities in winter weather. The tall sycamores sheltering the yards from the east winds made their long evening shadows fall across the road, when I saw the little hamlet of Plumpton would have to be my halting place for the night and at what better place than at Romanway Farm, the Turnbulls.

In these fine premises was a large stone trough on the sunny side of the huge yard which was quite inadequate to water the 120 cows which now use a modern system in the shippons, so Mrs Turnbull had converted it into a beautiful miniature garden. This trough is the focal point of the premises throughout the year, with its periodic displays of daffodils, geraniums or French marigolds, the whole giving disdain to the idea that farmyards must of necessity be messy places.

Over the meal and until time to retire we talked and I really think these two middle-aged folk were glad of someone else in the household, particularly with the children married and left home.

Up early to see some farming activities before leaving, I asked "How does the first beast know where to go?" when they were still ambling a quarter of a mile up the fields. The farmer replied that they will not feed anywhere about where they have recently fed for obvious hygienic reasons, if they can avoid it; and the offer of fresh, unpulled grass is better than that already sampled. Therefore they proceed to pasturage immediately beyond where grazed earlier. Fred sees to the moving of the electric fence a 'reach' further on every $1\frac{1}{2}$ hours and then returns to the farm.

Fred Baker, seventy-two and still a fine, able worker, decided when his wife died that he would rather continue working on this 'happy' farm to the mutual agreement of man and master. In giving an account of himself, he apologized for any possible spelling mistakes, since he left school so long ago, as "one becomes forgetful at seventy-two". I didn't find one, in the account very legibly written and readable.

There is a variety of tasks about a farm and monotony is avoidable, and the outdoor activity provides healthy living. Machines these days have taken much of the hard labour out of the various tasks, but when he first began, the farmer only possessed a grass mower so all harvesting was done by hand.

A happy feature of those days was his association with heavy legged horses which he loved, like other folk love pets. Being kind to his steeds, he got a full and willing response from them. From my own experience I recall the gentle thrust of soft, warm muzzles rummaging for sugar lumps, and the satisfying crunching sounds of the horses eating their oats. The strong tang of ammonia in a stable was a far healthier smell than the counterpart of diesel fumes from the soulless tractor, which Fred said he was sorry to see chugging about the land to replace his teams.

Farming is most profitable only on a big scale where machines can be used to capacity and make purchasing them a sound commercial proposition. Small farmers need other part-time work to make a livelihood, and gradually these small-holdings are disappearing with the land being added to larger farms.

Milking used to be a slavish job, just imagine milking 120 cows by hand. Now it is all done by electricity and stored in cooled tanks until fetched by bulk tankers and dispatched to all parts of the country.

Up in Cumberland where weather is unpredictable, hot weather is not now an indispensable part of harvesting since grass is turned into silage instead of hay, so that the self-feeding methods can be used.

What pleasanter country is there than Britain amongst

the farmlands in the growing seasons, when each holding is identifiable with its county? I left Romanway Farm out on the high fields looking away to Blencathra and the Lakeland Fells on 12 October, cool enough to compete with M6 traffic —three fields away, but at the leisured pace of 2½ miles in the hour I could see more than all the folk on the other trails. Along my way in ages past soldiers would tramp, and more recently farmers would bring in their produce—eggs, butter, cheese, hens or geese, on horseback, the men leading their horses to the market, and riding back probably with a few goods purchased in the town of Penrith.

Soon the close-walled streets dipped into the town centre revealing shopping properties old and new, then the castle ruin gaunt and repelling, probably once manned by the sentry whose body lay in a giant's grave 13 feet in length in the interesting old St Andrew's churchyard, and also a monument erected to a Robert Virtue, a former superintendent during the building of the Lancaster–Carlisle Railway who carried out his duties to the satisfaction of all under his jurisdiction with goodwill.

The red sandstone glowed on the church, which contained a fine mural showing 'Christ's agony in the garden'; next some attractive Tudor cottages, which are functional where one serves as a café.

High up, the Beacon Hill (937 feet) frowned down on Penrith, where in times past its watchers had been warned of approaching Scots long before the marauders had chance to raid. Now in more peaceful days only beacons of goodwill are lit to celebrate great occasions and so I left the place to continue with its marketing and pressed on towards Shap.

23 *The Backbone of England*

By the time I reached Shap in the dark, the gradual climb to its height above sea level of 852 feet had quite astonished me, for the steady ascent was imperceptible.

My way lay through the charming village of Lamont Bridge; a quieter place it is difficult to find, and I had no sooner crossed the bridge when some gypsy or squatters' caravans came into view. To pass them I walked backwards in mortal fear, facing four ferocious dogs, an Alsatian, and three curs which attacked me baring vicious fangs. Sweating in terror, I gradually escaped by inching from their territory until I passed by pleasant fields to Clifton, with its little church possessing a huge headstone to its porch 'straight from the ground', unworked by masons, the other stones being chosen to fit the natural curves in the main lintel. In the village a typical farmhouse of this Pennine region, built with indigenous stone mossy with age, had a building with a chamber reached with a stone stair; such convenient means of access, besides having great aesthetic appeal, also saves considerable space in a building. The village was one to linger in to enquire into its history, and questioning a woman of my age, a school's traffic warden, for information, she revealed she and her husband made model traction engines as their combined hobby.

The 54 inches by 22 inches 2-hundredweight traction engine had largely been made in the kitchen where annealing and silver soldering had been done by using three 5-pint blow lamps together, Mrs Wilson being very handy in moving the lamps where required. Where would one find many wives allowing three roaring blow lamps in their kitchens, or oily, greasy rags cluttered about, or the screech of hacksaws on metal, or the whirr of drilling machines with the messy waste tramping about the floor? This is happening in Clifton, with

Mr Wilson's patient and capable wife sawing spokes, filing, drilling holes and whatever else she can do to help him fulfil his life's ambition—to work on engines. Her desire is to steam up with anthracite fuel and drive one—her own!

Mr Wilson wrote that his interest had not been without difficulties, as when a boy, one weekend when the thresher was at a local farm, he and his friend bought a sheet of emery cloth and obtained his mother's brasso and rubbed and rubbed, to clean up the rusty parts, and obviously removed some of the paint. He remarked, it was as well they were in school that Monday morning when the engine driver saw what had happened.

I must add, their home looked less like an engineer's shop than any house I called in, it was like a palace and being regaled, off I set again—late!

Here again were 'spangles' of buildings around farmhouses and old troughs used as displays for begonias and nasturtiums. The houses faced south with buildings sheltering the yards except for an opening on the leeward side. 'Throughs' in the grey stone walls denoted the sound bonding of both sides of the work; there is never any buckling separation when throughs are seen projecting. The large grey stone slates, oak-pegged above the slate laths, seldom budge in a lifetime in fiercest gales, whereas blue slates and modern roofing materials would be torn away from the nails.

Steadily but surely ascending the long incline into colder air, the sky above me clouded darkly with a huge squadron of starlings homing to roost, and then a few minutes later a storm of starlings, ragged in flight, undetermined whether to stay out longer to the end of a glorious day. Then last of all, ten minutes later still, a shower of starlings, stragglers for the reason of remoter feeding than the rest and probably when reaching the homing trees would scarce find twigs to roost upon.

The Pennine reaches of northern parts are beautiful with bold masses and walls or hedgerows following undulating terrain, the air clean and biting giving a sharpness to detail miles away, not like the indefinitions of cities' demarcations and fug. I felt braced to take the last six miles and enjoy it, when I was stung to reality on my bare arm by some nettles hanging from Hackthorpe's police headquarters' garden—no complaints! The new portion to the old school had been carefully planned and executed to blend and make a nice building keeping apace with the modern trend compatible with the old.

As sombre shades of purples and browns heralded the night, a dog barked from the safety of his farm and kept his distance; and then a confused roar developed from the M6 traffic overhead on the crossing viaduct and a speeding train on its lonely line. Soon all was quiet but for the steady rhythm of my pacing as on I strode into the company of ghoulish pines. The eerie phantoms fronted some large limestone works, which with stark outline and few lights looked like a large dragon ready to pounce on me, breathing out smoke which joined the dark sky over the hills.

I was only four miles from the wild country of Haweswater and now in retrospect I regard this part of my journey as the loneliest stretch in all England. It was a delight eventually to see the twinkling lights of Shap, and none brighter than those of the 'Hermitage' where Mrs Jackson put on a sumptuous meal enough for the 'five thousand'.

After feasting, I was in good shape for the next morning when some snow had settled on the fells, and the keen air sharpened the wits. I bought a beret in the village, with no trouble, as every variety of shop in the long street displayed their many wares. Not less in numerical competition were the many large inns, which in many wild winters must have been filled to capacity with stranded passengers. Strangely on this nippy autumn day there were more gay gardens blooming than one would expect, and on I went straining with 'collar work' over the tops into the wilds. To miss Lakeland traffic through Kenal and beyond I purposely went eastwards a few miles and then strongly south again. I had wondered why Shap had so many shops and inns in such a remote and weird country, when I was told about the huge granite quarries nearby which for a century had a large influx of workers whose needs must be met.

The information kindly given by Mr A. L. Kirk indicated that geologists found iron and granite near Shap Fell about the time when the Thames Embankment was envisaged. Granite only was considered suitable for the project and none more favoured than 'Aberdeen'. Before finally deciding on this, other kinds were tested for strength, when a former Scottish quarryman who had moved to Penrith offered samples of Shap granite which proved 'second to none' in strength and colours also.

Shap received the order for the material, which by its merit won orders for bollards around St Paul's and work on the Stock Exchange. The granite, so pleasing in fleck, colour and polish, began to be used for monumental work, with the result that the products from this outlandish village became world famous. One renowned project using Shap granite is the lining of the Southampton docks, where limits on the proximity to the gates required an accuracy of four thousandths of an inch to avoid leakage.

This tough material needs tough men to cope with its quarrying and shaping and one can well imagine, with the influx of Scotsmen working amongst the untravelled men of Shap when first work began, that the lot of the foreman would not be easy to keep the peace. Now the firm employing experienced men and modern methods continues prosperously and agreeably, out on the wild land of hills and dales. To avoid main-road traffic I diverted by a steeply undulating superb narrow road through the village of Orton, yet, before reaching this spot in the wilds, to be saved the experience of being severed in two, I walked in the long grass as a tractor and trailer, bearing the overhanging sections of a large wooden shed, passed along the narrow lane into the beyond; it would meet no other traffic that day. It was a sad day for Orton, once Scar Overton, for the only folk about were three who were waiting to attend the funeral of a revered old villager.

These Pennine people, Mr and Mrs Gordon Coates, busy farming folk, gladly complied with my requests for information regarding the old market town where once fairs were held annually in Whit week. At these, horses, cattle, sheep, crockery and fancyware were sold. In the Market Hall built by the freeholders, tri-annually manorial courts are held and Orton boasts—as only one other village in the whole of England can—that the freeholders and landowners vote for and elect their own vicar.

The little Gothic church of All Saints has a carillon of eight bells which it is said were cast in Nottingham in 1529, indicating how important the locality was in those days.

I did observe on passing the large Hall, two carved lions 'guarding' the entrance, still faithfully from the year 1662. Orton too has had from ancient times strong religious attachments, the worshipping of Druids, then monks, and finally after the Anglicans the Nonconformists, the holy well named Ladywell being evidence of the trust in the Almighty for water in the area.

'Once upon a time' there lived an old woman in the area who was supposed to be a witch and who could foretell the future with such accuracy as to prophesy the coming of horseless carriages which would go over Loups Fell, and where now both the railway and the motorway pass.

This same woman met a farmer who had two sheepdogs, one young and the other old, which wanted to see a hare. The man asked where their wish could come true, so she directed him to a certain field where he would see one, but he must only allow the old one to give chase—just the old one!

Taking his dogs where directed, there sure enough was a hare, so he loosed the young dog to be certain he would catch it. When the farmer caught up with the dog there was no hare—but only the old woman who from that day always limped.

I left Orton to descend to Old Tebay and then climb again into New Tebay, just for a little practice for the 400-foot climb I was soon to negotiate. It is beautiful country, remote, with people 'down to earth', good-mannered, kind and generous. Here a formidable assemblage of brick houses with outside coalhouses looked like grim soldiers guarding the railway track between the giant hillsides over 1200 feet high. They are the dwellings of so many railway workers once needed to maintain and keep open the wild stretch of tracks in the Shap area; further, some men were much used in driving 'donkey' engines which assisted the not so powerful steam engines which plied with passengers or freight up the steep inclines, and now are obsolete by reason of the gigantic diesels able to master the gradients.

Of all the engineering wonders of my time in the construction of roadways, apart from the huge suspension bridges, here near Tebay is the situation, it is colossal. Literally the sides of mountains have been shaped to take the gradients out of the M6, allowing traffic to negotiate steady curves and 'levels' free from undulations. Never before have I seen greater evidence of Isaiah's truth "The crooked shall be made straight, and the rough places plain." The returfing and seeding have been done with such skill that the motorway seems as if it has ever been. It is to be seen to be believed—*but*—see it after climbing up the A685 towards Kendal, and carry a full haversack and two cameras, etc., then you'll need as many halts as I did, to afford opportunity to look back on that mighty chasm of moving automobile 'spiders' crawling on the long threads which gradually disappear into the distance.

This portion of the journey was second only to the Scourie–Kylesku Ferry 'leg' in straining every muscle; and as I descended on the other side of Grayrigg common, the tremendous scene stretched out beyond Sedbergh to the gigantic mass of Baugh Fell. (The next morning in sharp sunshine and frosty air gave me the most memorable sight ever in any of the Dales' country.) Still descending, I passed through the farmlands of the upper Lune Valley, seeing only one farmer and his dog, riding a tractor which did not stop to allow me to enquire for hospitality. Wearily along an old lane by Stocks Firbank I wandered, brushing the hedge to avoid a chance vehicle coming, when I knocked at a likely place, no one in, then another, same result—Heavens, shall I have to walk to Sedbergh? I thought, when I saw a woman on the steeply rising ground to a farm, whom I hailed. The woman about my age smiled in welcome to be addressed, but offered no hope at the farm: I could see why, for she had lost her right arm, the blouse sleeve being tucked neatly away. She replied that owing to the serious illness of her daughter-in-law in hospital, she was obliged to care for her two grandchildren, two boys; further there was her husband, and with other difficulties she felt unable or she would have gladly boarded me herself. Regretfully she said, "Oh Mister, I only wish I could oblige you, but I'll tell you how to get to another farm where they can take you in."

As I left her we shook hands—left-handed—when I felt a warmth of goodwill in her grip as we said goodbye. I ambled from the high yard and gradually lost myself between the high hedgerows—it was dusk. Shall I find the other farm before dark? I wondered, when the noisy approach of a car from behind made me thrust into the hedge. Its driver, an ageing man, told me to jump in, which I refused, until I knew he wished me to return to the farm on the hill.

"Oh, how kind of you both to consider helping me, but I'm sure your wife has more than enough to cope with, handicapped as she is."

"Who says she can't cope? She can do more wi' one arm than many women can wi' two."

I did as he commanded, put my gear in the back seat and we were soon in the yard, where the beaming farmer's wife stood in a welcoming attitude.

"Before you get out mester, let me ask you—can you put up with us being a bit untidy?"

"Of course, as long as I've a roof over my head and some good company I'll do fine."

"You'll get both," he said. "Our name's Armitstead, what's yours, mester?" he asked.

I told them, then his wife said, "Mr Kyme, I'm so glad you've returned, I just didn't know what to say when you first came into the yard, but after you left my husband and I discussed matters, and we agreed we could put the small boys in one bed, and so fix you up. Take your things off and I'll have a cup of tea ready in a minute; then if you'll agree, we can all dine together later," Mrs Armitstead told me.

Having seen the lads to bed, Mrs Armitstead went into the kitchen where soon I heard the sounds of pot washing, which I asked to be allowed to do to save her this double-handed chore.

"Oh, no thanks, Mr Kyme, you're tired, rest yourself and talk with my husband," and so it was. This tough man with a great use of the vernacular, revealed his interest in good books, and talked of Milton and Shakespeare and of the preparation of a family tree, going as far back as possible; telling me of the many variations in spelling their name. Of course there are ancesters of any family who have stood out from the rest for some particular reasons, therefore when he came to discussing his own history about farming, he came to a halt, and asked, "Would you like to hear how my missus lost her arm?"

"Well, it has concerned me, but I had felt it no business of mine. Why, Mr Armitstead?"

"You don't mind me telling him how you came by your accident, Mary?"

"No, you can tell him Tom," she replied.

The farmer then told me how they were getting on reasonably well on their hillside holding, mainly rearing sheep along with a few cattle and poultry. He decided to employ a young man, on the basis of helping a person who would benefit by outdoor life since he had suffered a serious mental illness. He appeared to have progressed satisfactorily and could work unattended. However, one day the farmer told his wife he would have to increase his stock of sheep, which would entail him going to a distant auction when he would return next day. Mrs Armitstead expressed fears of being left alone as the young man had leered at her whenever her husband was distant from the farm. Her husband tried to reassure her, saying he would be harmless and so left for the sale.

The young man, seeing him depart, immediately went to the barn for a gun he had hidden and at the first opportunity of seeing the woman about her chores, shot her. She ran for her life, seriously injured, to a neighbouring place. Eventually the young man was captured and placed under special care; while the unfortunate woman had to have her right arm amputated.

Worse was to follow, for on her return home to try and rehabilitate herself in her disablement, delayed shock resulted in serious blindness following. The doctor yielded under pressure for the farmer to get the best specialist attention, for he said he did not wish them to spend their hard-earned capital on what appeared to be inevitable tragedy.

Treatment and faith resulted in Tom Armitstead receiving a letter written in 'gold': "Dear Tom, I'm coming home and will see you soon", the shaky but beautiful handwriting done left-handed by a woman who had been on the verge of total blindness.

Here were two people who had turned adversity into a triumph, helping other people and thus pushing their own problems into the background. They went on to tell me that in the seventeenth century, George Fox preached from their hillside; and that Ruskin visited Kirkby Lonsdale, as also the renowned artist J. M. W. Turner, and definitely I must see Ruskin's view before making Ingleton by nightfall.

A frost had sharpened the atmosphere during the night, and the clear-cut shapes of the mountains next morning stood out against the clear sky a duck-egg blue. The farmer would not let me go until he had given me a little run up the valley to take photographs. We had the fields and riverside to ourselves except for a few hens which wandered from little hutches near the farmsteads. "It's round here where true nature lovers wander at weekends when they want to escape from the towns—there's nowt like t'Lune Valley," he remarked. Across, the hillsides began to catch the fierce sunlight and little plumes of chimney smoke rose straight into the windless sky, then beasts began to meander downhill from their shippons, the milking done, and I noted a gleam in Mr Armitstead's eyes as he asserted: "There yonder is our daughter's farm, we can always see what's going on at one farm or the other, and they can see our place; it's nice when you can be helpful to each other when you're in need."

He took me back to Stocks Farm, where I took the photographs of him and his wife with their well-trained dog, and left never to forget the homely welcome I received in their tidy farmhouse.

I was away down the narrow lane, in and out of the little church and the graveyard where on a stone was chiselled, "I will lift up mine eyes unto the hills", and soon reached the valley bottom with the rapturous sight of Middleton Fell before me. Autumn colours on the trees—still leaf-bearing —and the Lune meandering on its way to Lancaster provided a living canvas. The steep-sided fells fresh green from new growth caused by the nibbling sheep, and nature's efforts to give fresh yield, made the hillsides appear to be covered with lawn grass. There are the little places Middleton, Barbon and Casterton all little gems of freedom from the new craze of concrete and glass monstrosities, and somewhere about any of these places can one settle down, and sit before an easel and capture more happy 'memories' for the album or art competition. This valley of the Lune is so superb that before I would leave it I did an extra mile by sauntering around Kirkby Lonsdale to see the view Turner painted, and described as one of the loveliest scenes in England. To preserve this glorious view, land has been purchased for the public's enjoyment by one Alexander Pearson, and I can think of nothing nicer in those parts than to sit near the church and look across the river meadows away to the fells and the soaring clouds. This was my good fortune, it was just such a day as I tramped through; it could have been raining.

There is the old cross—unfortunately smashed by recent vandalism—and the beautiful old buildings adjacent, suitable for anyone to make a good canvas or two, but unfortunately photographers would not be so lucky in making ideal pictures by reason of parked vehicles. Probably local people want their vehicles near at hand instead of in a distant car park; it is a pity however that this one particular spot cannot be left clear for visitors to see this vicinity unspoilt by modern transport. Kirkby Lonsdale is only one of such beautiful places where it would be nice if only such gems of architectural merit could be left free from all vehicles say for two hours at some part of each day. It could bring in pedestrian traffic to the cafés and shops after folk had had a saunter round.

The market is a delight also, full of local people with a good mixture of visitors even in mid October; in fact anyone motoring up the M6 wanting a worthwhile break before proceeding to the Lake District or Scotland should have a rest by turning off at Junction 36 and spending a time at Kirkby Lonsdale, if only to see Ruskin's view alone; incidentally the residents are charming and helpful people.

The day was now in decline and cooler, and still six miles to go, so I 'dug' into the journey with speed, exhilarated by treasured sights of mountains seen in now familiar country. One can't see the gradual mystic change of appearance of Ingleborough when riding swiftly: to me in the fading light

Above: A model traction-engine made by a man and his wife at Clifton. The camera case in the foreground gives an idea of its size.
Below: Pennine country at Nateby, near Appleby

I was boarded by these fine Pennine folk, the Armitsteads

In the Lune valley (the M6 to Tebay is hidden by the tree)

A wet day in Settle

The Leeds–Liverpool Canal at Gargrave

These washing lines at Brighouse prevented a lorry driver from using the road

Above: Sheffield's Abbeydale Works Industrial Museum – a national prize piece of restoration – has been put in working order mainly by the great efforts of a retired enthusiast, Humphrey Nowill, here shown inspecting the huge waterpower-driven wheels. *Below:* Monument commemorating the repeal of the Corn Laws, in Dronfield

Pike-Watts sculpture at Ilam, executed by Sir Francis Chantrey

Lower Birchett Farm, Dronfield

Wilfred Alton, a retired miner. In the background is the defunct colliery winding gear at Williamthorpe

its huge mass looked like a guarding sphinx, and all the other contours seemed like a defensive wall against the phantoms of the approaching night. Just before closing, the shop at Cowan Bridge provided an ice-cream, and information as to where in the village is the cottage adjacent to the bridge where the Brontë sisters stayed a few months not far from the sea at Morecambe, and the lofty fells to the east.

The cold air cooled my brow as I left the village form, and soon the turquoise sky to the west changed to the same sombre inky blue of the east, where mountain guardians merged their outlines in the sky, indefinably. I was alone, until the twinkling lights of Ingleton greeted me after a perfect day.

The little town of Ingleton has always been important to me from the days when its famous railway arches and mountainous background were shown on art posters in railway stations. It still lives up to the standards of good service, and a healthier setting for the energetic could not be desired.

There's Ingleborough (2373 feet), potholes, Gaping Ghyll, waterfalls, and splendid sights of stalactites and stalagmites in the caves—more than enough of Pennine hill country, but not for me this time as I set out again in changed conditions of cold, clammy hill mists, that later turned into dousing rain.

There was not the remotest chance of seeing Morecambe Bay, the visible limits being the sheep grazing on the wide spaces of short, cropped grass on unfenced road pasturage and the dim outline of the sphinx of Ingleborough guarding from marauders of the north.

Squelching along through moorlands, onwards through Clapham to the frowning forehead of crags and trees above Giggleswick, I visited the old house café, being the only visitor, and ordered soup and coffee and watched the steam from beaker and dish drift forcibly towards me by reason of draughts through casement windows.

I dived out (thankful for the respite) under the sorrowful trees that hang down from the limestone scar and into Giggleswick Village on a rainy day—but photography was hopeless from a sheltered place for twenty vehicles of every description were lined up in a crocodile to collect boys ready for a weekend at home.

Who wants to see me today, to give me information for a million and more strides? I thought. No one. So by sheer resolution I then squelched into Settle, that Mecca of farmers and marketeers from all around for miles—a sublime place in good weather. But ugh! I stood under a shop entrance and watched the rain pelt down on empty car tops, their owners surely regaling themselves in every single café.

We all know what a magnificent centre Settle is for Yorkshire Dales' tours and caves, but I wracked my brain for another approach to life in a little town, and decided to take a photograph of Settle on a wet day. Impossible in such a deluge and glum weather to hold the camera still enough, I went into a ladies' wear shop to the astonishment of the two young lady assistants to borrow some steps on which to clamp my camera. They were courteous indeed and gave me a welcome cup of tea, and allowed me to remove my sodden anorak. Just in the very act of 'shooting', a middle-aged man came into the porch and asked what I was up to, who from his tone of voice could hardly believe me; finding I was seriously doing as I had informed him, Richard Moore of the Settle market place, who has three shops, told me the story of the business and showed me all departments of his prosperous concern.

In 1894 John Moore, who was a Westmorland farmer's son, decided to go in for a drapery business, and served an apprenticeship in Sheffield, but before setting up he looked around various towns before deciding on Settle. He was only three miles from home where he first displayed wares in the little shop and had cycled there to open up for 8 a.m. His capital was very small, but he hoped all day for custom, sitting on the stairs listening for the door opening while he ate his sandwiches. By the time 10 p.m. came and the shop closed, he had for his whole day's takings one shilling payment by a customer for three collars.

The young fellow cycled home dejectedly fearing ruin, wondering what to do to save face and his hard-earned capital. He decided to advertise, and from that action began to do business.

Later, John's son Richard exhibited the same resolution in running his three-shop concern, this day, in 'sorrowing' Settle as we dashed from door to door for me to be proudly introduced to his staff. This done, watched by Mr and Mrs Moore, with equal resolution I plunged into the weeping, disconsolate streets, to make my way on the suicidal narrow road to Long Preston—no footpaths and the scurrying lorries and cars dashing homewards for the weekend made it most frightening.

Sodden yet again, I tried my fortune for accommodation but without success, six places, seven——nine, tried persuasion in desperation and went into a public house a second time to eat and drink what was provided and contributing to the most extensive use of the vernacular I ever recall.

"Good evening Mr Landlord, could you serve me a meal, please?" I asked.

"Nay lad, tha carn't ger owt 'ere, my missis is badly."

"Well, I've tried nine places and can't get any food. What do you suggest? I'm desperate."

"Tha can 'ave sum pies and peas warmed up, they'll none teck long. Can tha wait?"

"Coffee, please?"

"Nay lad, Ah 'aven't time to du thi eny. Tha wants to get a pint o' ale darn thi, then tha'll be as reight as a fiddle."

I did as he advised.

Meanwhile customers stood with one elbow on the counter with a hand apiece grasping their pots, all the time ogling me from head to foot. I did wonder why pint pots had handles since nobody ever used them.

The landlord and his worthies watched me struggle into my wet outer garment and fasten my hood and finally separate myself from them and the blazing fire to go out into the bleak world. I had traipsed enough up and down Long Preston to know it blindfolded, and soon found an old barn doorway with a large lintel to shield me from the rain and wind, and stood forlornly wondering where to go. The place seemed dead for some time, when I noticed a limping man pushing a laden cycle, silhouetting himself against the street lighting; he must have had a keen eye to have spotted me. He asked why I was standing there, and being informed he went home to discuss matters; in no time Mr and Mrs

Harrison—school caretakers—had taken me into their lovely home.

After a night's good rest and fine fare, I was soon amongst the rolling hills trekking towards Skipton, through Hellifield, where on one fierce night of a tremendous gale, a railway guard noticed the loss of some new cars blown clean off the transporter train; for such can be the weather in these uplands of Yorkshire.

It is remarkable that at about this stage of my journey, even in October, there seemed to be a notable change in the hedgerows and woodlands; foliage seemed to be more profuse and tree stature of major proportions. Cottages and houses possessed style and charm besides providing accommodation. Wall fences here and there vied with hedgerows and gave grace to field shapes with curves and angles like some great jigsaw puzzles; it is heartening to note that dry-stone walls are being used as road boundaries to new thoroughfares in various parts of the north.

At Conniston Cold I asked a young man with a broken arm (chestnutting), "Why Conniston Cold?" He didn't know, and the other chestnut collectors neither; however Mr and Mrs Gomersall showed me their old schoolhouse with its stone-flagged flooring and bacon-side hooks in the ceilings. Out at the rear of their one-time farmhouse there was a sizeable croft, which could give credence to the statement that it may have been a cold harbour for penning sheep which would be brought down from the hills early on in the year to be in safe quarters for lambing time. This little village still retains its century-old appearance, for there have been no additions; for how long 'progress' can be kept at bay to prevent spoiling this little place is a question.

I left these proud villagers and their white-fenced cottages bordered with flowers and continued towards Gargrave with a large village green and stream, now becoming known to the canal-cruising community who have attractive fields to pass through, and for excitement a fair number of locks to negotiate while baffled with the horns of a dilemma—for a large herd of cows browsed near one lock sufficiently close to fall in. This charming stretch of the Leeds-Liverpool Canal competes with the little stream which passes through Gargrave, which is a splendid place to draw in for a time to browse around, or trail one's feet in the water.

Here is a gentle introduction to the industrial north, for the large factory for powder preparations dominates the lower end of the village; and somehow, as I nosed into the long journey through the industrial landscapes, I felt my bag to weigh a stone heavier—my heart stayed northwards.

24 *Yorkshire is Not All Cricket*

SOME outsiders consider Yorkshire both as a county and as a people to be grim; there is in England's largest county enough of it to have a stern independence, and its people have forthright characters which leave no doubt about intentions of conducting business. They will carry their independence to great limits some would call ridiculous, such as to field a truly Yorkshire born and bred cricket team against the Australians. Many still have a propensity for being careful in spending, which trait comes from money being hard earned. They will not readily accept strangers, but having done so, will prove staunch friends.

Cricket was over and done with, as I elbowed through Skipton, once Sheepton, where the Saturday market thrived in selling anything and everything, and folk from the surrounding hill hamlets seemed jammed into the spacious main thoroughfare. Two old farmers—with their sheepdog companion—noticed me and nodded in goodwill. I could have turned off by the stolid church and taken the road to Bolton Abbey on the Wharfe and had an exciting time even in the dull weather, but I forged ahead on towards Bradford by the long road to Kildwick where the mellowed stone church stands high off the corner, with its superb rounded and worn steps leading to the long path. The edifice stands there with a benign aspect to the south-west, offering peace to the one-time red rose antagonists over the hills. Surely all worshippers or agnostics in the old days of 'all work and no play' must have enjoyed the beautiful churches as a pleasant alternative from the huge rectangular mills and gaunt chimneys; and the rich music, as a diversion from the row and rattle of spindle and fliers. Kildwick church always catches the eye on a trip 'up north'.

Inside ten minutes I called it enough, and visited the kindly Allens who took me to church next morning where I heard my former minister Rev. David Milner preach in Sutton Baptist church.

Christians are an unpredictable folk for they upset all my calculations for a quick move on after the service. My baggage was left in the church and then a car whisked me to the hilltops around Keighley and as quickly down again betweenwhiles ridding me of the idea that mill towns are 'all muck and money' and dark satanic mills. All around, the high ridges and broad valleys form the water-gathering grounds that furnish the many mills with water for their processing; yet besides, on those high tops I regained the freedom of the hills where there's sighing grass and keen air, singing larks and calling curlews. Times are better, living standards have improved and it's not all bed and work, so there will be some who will go 'on the tops' for a break at weekends instead of going to bingo halls.

The Bell family gave me the freedom of their house where a truly Yorkshire dinner was served up by grannies—there was more than enough, even though I was an unexpected guest. Then for my entertainment daughter and son not yet left school played a duet on piano and trumpet; it was all first class, and when I was returned to get my baggage and recommenced my walking, this sociability gave me a great fillip.

Now for miles I would be in built-up areas passing between old stone dwellings, public houses and large Nonconformist churches which seem to keep in competition for splendour and flamboyance both inside and out. Built by prosperous mill-owners most of them, and filled to capacity each Sunday in the late Victorian era. Filled with a conglomeration of fashionably dressed wealthy folk in some pews, and coarse-clothed, down at heel, hungry, pinched-faced people in the others.

Some folk went to worship, and some just to be seen from the boss's pew that they were there, to keep the favour of having work in the mill. And some would go to sing in the notable choral music, particularly the *Messiah* and *Elijah*. These chapel walls 'speak' the history of Bradford, Brighouse and Huddersfield, showing now by their sadly depleted congregations that improved conditions for work and better payment have not necessarily indicated the desire of people to show thankfulness in public worship.

I went on, between better types of modern villas, each with a front and rear, garden and garage, homes of business folk living 'out of town'. How I longed for an oasis of somewhere possible for a fellow to take his dog let loose from the lead when I suddenly saw a flash of sunlight on water down a side turning. This revealed the little lake adjacent to old Riddlesden Hall, a gem of the architecture that reminds one of Haworth and the Brontë country. It is a relief when such old places escape the bulldozer and continue to remind us of originality of style and fitness to withstand the dales' weather. I left two young lovers under the coach house still trying to make up from their tiff and went on, but not for long, I was hungry, and sat on a wall, looking up at an old quarry that broke the building line of dwellings and had my 'break'.

A middle-aged man turned up from the roadway sauntering through the gorse and bracken and gradually disappeared; but a few minutes later there was a great flutter of pigeons which wheeled about the sky at great speed, glad to be free from the hut I had not noticed. I thought to myself what diversity of interests we people have who see more in life than just working and eating. Some I had the privilege of meeting were councillors, others artistic, some hobbyists making things with great precision, and there was this fellow absorbed in the pleasure of watching his homing pigeons, and who would fondle each in turn hoping one day there might be a top bird amongst them. Moving on and looking back occasionally, I could see the fellow watching the frenzied birds plunging and soaring, ringed with gold as they flew into the fierce evening sun dipping low into the leaden clouds near the horizon. To him they would be better than pure gold a solid and inanimate element; what price has the grace of movement, what pile of heaped gems would counterpoise the exhilaration of freedom? He would wander up twice daily, and in his working hours in the rowdy mill when for a moment things would be going well his thoughts would fly to the loft and his birds. Who said: Pigeons; messy things, the bane of our cities?

I could see him no longer for my elevation now made his person fuse with the gloom of the quarry, and so progress had to be made before dark. Bradford is surrounded by hill country as I soon realized keeping west of the city, and intermittently there would be modern roads and dwellings, then old roads with stone-cobbled footpath entries, stone pavings and long rows of squat houses. Next morning seeing more of such areas, much demolition was in progress, but where will it cease? I would urge on behalf of we few conservationists that Bradford will for perpetuity preserve such a street replete with old gas lamps, that visitors may see what a working-class area looked like in the late nineteenth century.

The Rev. David Milner had raced home from Sutton, told his wife of a marathon walker who would be their guest later in the evening, and both had prepared excellent welcome on my arrival. Having relaxed, we talked of Bradford as the gateway to the Dales, the place where a spade is called a spade with no equivocation. It just would appear to be so, for there are those who hail from Bradford who are in politics and trades unionism who speak with conviction and forthrightness, namely Mrs Barbara Castle, and Vic Feather. Dennis Healey also is a respected parliamentarian; and furthermore the arts are well represented by Delius with his dreamlike music, and Henry Moore by modern sculptures. Yet one more with a name of renown distinguished for his prolific and excellent writings, and talent for public speaking is J. B. Priestley.

On my way out towards Huddersfield, David escorted me a while, when we threaded through back streets and great mills, now defunct from their original purposes, but currently employed as huge warehouses. The fact of seeing these mills led him to mention Titus Salt, whose benefactions are well known in him founding the model village of Saltaire. This village of nicely planned houses and roads was an innovation of Salt's time whereby he provided beautiful homes for his work people, so that rather than being just pawns for completing work schedules, they received cultural benefits also. From such an experiment in improving the standards of the workers who universally were at one time underpaid, Titus Salt began a crusade which has continued to the present time.

This talented mill-owner's son was able to commence his philanthropy by accruing great prosperity through his initiative with some wool he observed lying in a Liverpool warehouse. He found the stuff was considered useless by other mill-owners, and so offered cheap to be rid of it. On taking a sample back to Bradford and experimenting with it, he eventually succeeded in weaving the material alpaca, named from the animal which gives the wool. Naturally he emptied the warehouse, and developed a very profitable business from the venture. The great feature of this undertaking was that the mill-owners passed many of the benefits of their initiative on to the work people, thus developing still greater production from a contented and appreciative labour force.

My companion returned home as I pressed on through more cobbled streets towards Brighouse, where all I had ever known of the place was of its reputable brass band. Brighouse and Rastrick, treated in the singular in music, is a power to be reckoned with at such places as Bellevue contests, or in the open valleys of Saddleworth competitions. It makes the blood stir to hear the staccato notes from trombones playing 'Mephistopheles' being re-echoed from the hillsides of Uppermill and Dobcross.

Here it was, mainly stone built; clean, with a tidily kept municipal garden cared for by someone interested in its presentation. Large carpet mills with the appearance of a good prosperous turnover, together with tidy streets and long rows of well-kept houses, made the impression on me that Brighouse was not just an adjunct to the famous band. It had made the band, and the technical college, and the operatic society; it surely is the nicest mill town in all the vast concourse of weaving communities.

But what's all this? There atop of a street was a lorry with an infuriated driver gesticulating and waving his hands in great frustration, because he could not get down the street since so many women had hung their washing out across the thoroughfare. He was furious, "Nobody bothers," he grumbled. The wind made the hanging garments flutter, as very young children bobbed in and out amongst the un-smirched flags of domestic Monday mornings. I knew it: when my journey would take me out of the built-up streets there would be some weather.

Huddersfield is just a junior Bradford in appearance, with many signs of redevelopment and modern buildings. There are outlets to wild moorland or meadows and woods, just the place for work and leisure. Famous for its bespoke tailoring and engineering, particularly for marine valves; and there are good educational facilities. It now began to pour with clammy wet rain when flagstones and cobbles shone with motley patterns, fanciful, opposed to the murky blackness of night creeping on. I had known Huddersfield before, for the generosity of one man in particular. I was a lone student in the Technical College, culling what knowledge could be gained from any source, as for my particular training there was no set course. However one night I had a forge working and irons heating, and periodically removed one to forge it to shape when I was startled on looking round to see a fellow watching me. We addressed each other as I continued to forge away.

"Young man," he said, "you don't mind if I show you how to do this in the accepted way?"

"I'd be grateful," I said, as I gave him my hammer.

He laid it on the anvil, removed his coat, rolled up his immaculate shirt sleeves, watched the metal heat up, then put the glowing iron on the anvil, and shaped it whilst giving me terse comments on the procedure. He then watched me and finally left, with a pleasant "Goodnight". His action put the hallmark on Huddersfield for me—he was the college principal.

To the task, I walked on, in the direction of Sheffield, two days away, and asked at first one place and another for accommodation and found none after many enquiries. Sodden through, and reluctantly about to turn back into the town, chafing under the rudeness and inhospitable remarks of one poor soul who should have learned better manners, I took one chance more for information leading to hotel accommodation, public house, or ordinary dwelling, when the silhouette of a man in a lighted window afforded me an opportunity of an enquiry.

"I can't hear very well, step inside while I ask my wife what you want to know," he said. She listened and then remarked, "Well, have a cup of tea and take your wet things off, then we can talk about where you can go." And yet another school caretaker, Mr Hill and his wife, afforded me a great northern welcome at Fenay Bridge.

Off again on a familiar road, by the bare, short-cropped grassy fields not one beast or sheep appeared anywhere and flood-waters poured through joints and gaps in walls from the sodden land into the road. Then, as can happen in hilly country, strong winds developed and quickly blew the clouds away, revealing the weak blue sky of the fading year.

A thrilling moment arrived at a small hamlet, when by sheer ingenuity in using some stones I managed, without wading, to get into a telephone box and phoned my sister and her husband to say where I would be if they were able to come and meet me. Alone on the high Pennine road with great vistas of bleak fields and moors, the wet town roofs of Penistone shone in the weak sunshine, and little farms, with outbuildings, looked like guarding shepherds with their dogs supervising their colonies in the draughty peaklands.

Then from the distance a car appeared, so small that no colour was discernible, until, as it proceeded, there was no need to scrutinize, for it stopped and its two occupants came damp-eyed to welcome me back home. They were, of course, my sister Elsie and my brother-in-law, the Austins, for whom I had tramped the quickest route back to be at their ruby wedding at the weekend.

For a while I was accompanied and then went on alone on the heights about the Don Valley, and halted at Thurgoland, at the local shop. The matronly owner asked, "Where have you come from, mister?"

"Madam, you won't believe me if I tell you."

Like most women her inquisitiveness prevailed until she found out, and said, "Let me get Mr Briggs to interview you for a story for the Barnsley paper," and having complied with the request, I asked the retired school teacher for an item in his experience which related to service in a Church of England school.

The local vicar had come to verify that Mr Briggs had instructed his pupils in religious education, which had been concerning the journeyings of the Israelites into Canaan, described as "a land flowing with milk and honey". Not readily obtaining an answer to his question, one bright lad saved the situation with his logical conclusion to "Yes boy, what would Canaan be like?" He answered, "Sticky, sir!"

Then came Wortley, a superb little 'halt' with its little peakland church and stone-built cottages, followed by the high road to Sheffield by Grenoside. Eastward and westwards wonderful panoramas spread for tremendous distances, and if I had cycled eastwards there would never have been a hill giving cause to dismount right to the coast. With field glasses, one would see easily the great Wentworth Mansion and Sir Walter Scott's Conisbrough, and Hooton Roberts church where once I sat outside to hear the hymn tune chimed by the clock. There were, out in the mosaic of fields and villages, little factories and collieries sending up whiffs of steam and smoke, but next the road I tramped along were farmers, with their potato spinners loosing the tubers for the eager youngsters to bag, during their West Riding potato picking holidays.

To westwards the bright sun shone fiercely over the Don Valley and Oughtibridge where my first childhood recollections began; and still further beyond, the white-rimmed clouds towered above the uplands of the 2000-foot Howden and Derbyshire peaklands. Before descending into Sheffield, I filled my lungs with the bracing air for this was the end of a spur of the Pennines; and no breeze again would invigorate me similarly until those from off the Channel at Dover.

How rightly spoke Ruskin who said, "Sheffield is an ugly picture in a golden frame"! It was; but now I would take him to task, for in these days, great progress has been made in cleaning public buildings, which, free from industrial grime, are now beautiful features of a great and progressive city. There is no English city comparable with Sheffield, which offers so many facilities and possesses rich heritages of historic interest in halls and mansions set in proximity to moorlands or spacious riverside parks. The call of the lapwing and the grouse are to be heard inside its boundary and from its highest elevations one can see Lincoln Cathedral on a clear day.

The city is in the southernmost part of England's largest county, its citizens epitomizing the characteristics of all Yorkshiremen: they are careful in spending, but lavish in generosity, particularly so to sportsmen receiving the takings of a benefit match together with a collection.

The city's workers have always been renowned for industry, and formerly, many died prematurely, for much of the processing of Sheffield's products in the past caused serious health troubles, particularly grinders' disease. Now with modern methods of production there are not such hazards, and personnel produce cutlery, tools, and steels dispatched the world over.

Typical of the men who prefer to be their own master were the one-time gaffers, or 'little mesters', who would employ a few people and do one particular branch of the cutlery trade such as blanking, grinding, polishing, handling, casemaking and despatch, a different firm doing each particular job.

In former times the streams down the several valleys on the outskirts of the city supplied water power for little factories, and dams were made to store water against droughts, 'to keep wheels turning'. One such factory called the Abbeydale Industrial Hamlet, before its revival into a superb working museum, formerly made scythes.

This former factory with its workers' cottages and foreman's house, possesses a number of workshops and a large forge, on which the city spent some worthwhile money upon to repair all the buildings. However no firm would give an estimate to put the now defunct machinery in working order, and only such places as the blacksmiths' shops could indicate where some of the processes were formerly done.

In 1966 a city education organizer interested in conservation retired and decided that he would fully restore the whole concern to a working museum, which took him and other volunteers until 1970 to complete. This project received national acclaim, and gained for Humphrey Nowill a deserved M.B.E.

When this energetic man took over the task to make the huge wheels and axles turn again, the heavy rotten timber remains and metal segments had collapsed into the sump where the bottom half of the tremendous driving wheel formerly turned. For a man, no longer young, to rescue parts of what was left for probable use again, was a dangerous task, and to retrieve the decayed timbers for reassembly, so that some assessment could be made of the former mechanism, needed great patience, skill and effort.

When I found this enthusiast, to take his photograph, I was guided to his location by the loud whacks of his sledge-hammer, beating large steel wedges into the wooden axle of the cogged wheel, to prevent any slackness and ensure even running. I am convinced it was sheer willpower that urged him to keep striking blows while working from the narrow wall position, where many a younger man would have required a scaffold.

Leaving the city, up the steep road to Dronfield my home town, my mind centred upon Britain's greatest sculptor Sir Francis Chantrey who grew from a farm lad to be a wealthy and famous artist, befriended by many great people. He was born in 1781 at Norton on the city's outskirts, and as a small schoolboy could be seen looking in stone walls for any medium to practise on with bits of steel or knives.

From drawing and painting which exhibited his great talent at an early age, he decided to apply himself to sculpture, and produced speaking likenesses of his sitters, which brought him great fame and demands upon his talent. In spite of honours he kept his humility, and deeply showed his affection for his mother by frequently writing to her and having goods delivered to her cottage. Upon her death, he did not travel the great distance from London for her funeral, for he said that he had looked after her while she lived so she needed no more respect from him now she was gone.

His most beautiful works show such great tenderness and grace in the limbs and features of the figures that one could almost see them breathe. One such is the Pike Watts Memorial Group at Ilam church, Dovedale; and the most famous of all his works is the beautiful group *The Sleeping Children*, in Lichfield Cathedral, which causes some who see it to leave in tears. The prototype of the latter is at Norton, and can be lifted by one hand, therefore one can imagine the superb skill of Chantrey needed in making the posy in the child's hand.

He died at sixty, and but for his desire to be interred in his father's grave he would have been buried in Westminster Abbey.

My excitement was keen on approaching home still on my way south, when in spite of a shocking wet evening developing, Roger Redfern my author friend came and escorted me back the last few miles to Dronfield wanting to carry my pack, which I would not allow. It was great to be home seeing again Dora my wife, and Andrew and Sheila—but one member of the family, Robbie our sheepdog collie, did everything but eat me. Thankfully I had made it in readiness for the ruby wedding.

25 *Mines and Mansions*

DRONFIELD, my home town, is just inside the border of north-east Derbyshire, and shortly will have completed the finest residential housing scheme in England. It is situated in a valley running north and south between pleasant hillsides, with the River Drone meandering sluggishly to join the Rother.

It has always been a place of importance, to be judged by the period when it possessed only 7,000 occupants but twenty-seven public houses, not only catering for the local people's thirst, but to offer hospitality to visitors en route from south or north.

Its main industrial pursuit for some centuries until my own days, was the making of edge tools for farming and household use, such as hedging bills, hooks, scythes, sickles and hatchets, the most infamous of the last being the very axe used to decapitate Charles I.

However, today a long-established business continues to make spades, shovels and forks, which go out the world over. In the days of its founders there was considerable civil unrest bordering on riot, and Dronfield was smouldering, since the working classes were underpaid. Echoes of troubles in Sheffield resulted in a boiler explosion in the Shovel Works one Sunday morning. Mr Lucas, the works' owner, and others, hearing the report gave chase on horseback to catch the perpetrators whom they found on the moors. The men were then gaoled in Chesterfield, pending trial.

Friends of these men, hearing where the fellows had been arrested, got drunk, and feigned such to the point of being of disorderly conduct, until they too, were put in the same gaol, and being so many, some had to be put with those who caused the explosion. This situation had been planned, to free the men from the serious charge for a lesser one which would soon obtain them release.

The friends, following the horsemen, noticed the place of capture, later hid some poaching equipment, and were able to tell the prisoners to say that they had been poaching, and, seeing the approaching horsemen, hid their tackle in the moorland grough, hoping to avoid being charged.

The prisoners were charged with the explosion, and thus gave the alibi, stating where their equipment could be found; therefore the case was then deferred until this fact could be proved. When police checked this location and brought the poaching gear to court as proof of their statement, the prisoners only received the lighter sentence and soon their freedom.

The Lucas family had another factory for iron moulding, which made spindles and fliers for work in the Lancashire cotton mills, but wherever firms made these parts, serious trouble was caused by them breaking, due to the brittle nature of the cast iron used. Much investigation had gone into a means of reducing the fragile nature of cast intricate work, when finally success came to this firm in inventing malleable iron about 1790.

Also in the middle 'eighties, with the great civil unrest problem smouldering, there was one manufacturer with strong liberal political views and sympathies with the low-paid workers, who decided that he would support the poorer classes in their fight against the militia if the occasion arose. Paul Jackson closed his edge tool works from normal trade, and had his sympathizers manufacture round iron balls with four inserted pegs sharpened and arranged so that when thrown, the contraptions would rest on three pegs, leaving one sticking uppermost to cause horses to stumble and dislodge their riders. Then the local defenders, prying through the loopholes in their sheet metal shutters, would see to fire on the aggressors confused by falling. Paul Jackson was much respected by the lower classes, and generally, was appointed as an acting policeman for the area.

Dronfield has a magnificent parish church with Gothic arches and Norman columns, and boasts the second largest parish church east window in England. It is the glorious focal point from vantage positions from all the surrounding hills, and so inspired J. M. W. Turner to stop in his touring to paint a picture of this notable building. St John the Baptist's has superlative examples of woodcarving by the Tideswell master craftsman Advent Hunstone, and to see this alone is worthy of a visit. Older carvings on pew ends are beautifully symbolic of the church's function—such as the impressive eagle, and the pelican pecking her breast that her young may continue to live though she dies—thus representing the highest strivings towards heaven, and the sacrifice of Christ for His people. There are excellent brasses also.

In the town are some fine old buildings dating from the sixteenth century, especially Chiverton House. A very attractive monument relating to the repeal of the Corn Laws occupies a place in an enclave of stone-built property, fortunately being conserved in the surrounding modern-built territory.

Around this monument in former days markets were held, and on the 'Statis' (Statute or Hiring Fair) being due, farm labourers and maids would stand near the Manor House wall and await hiring, to begin their labours from 1 March, the commencement of the farming year. Hired people would receive a 'fastening penny', to clinch the deal with their future employers.

Dronfield's bounds stretched into remote areas of small hamlets remaining in the control of the small township, where the parochial records were kept in the church chest. In those days agricultural work had not extended to the hilltops, and therefore high ground was heather covered and supported a large bee population. These insects not only produced honey for the local population, but wax also, which was used for making candles. It is a pleasant thought that Dronfield's house lights and fires of those times were lit with holy flames, since the poorer folk, having no flints or tinder, would go to the church for worship, and on leaving would have their lantern candles lit from the altar candles, and then on returning home would kindle their faggots indirectly from the holy source, the altar flame.

Amongst the inhabitants of this town who have had influence upon people was a local practitioner, Dr Fletcher, who bought the Manor House and then bequeathed it for the use of the local council. I remember him driving the first car I had ever seen, and this furiously over the dusty limestone roads, creating a great pother, and scattering scratching hens wildly from its path. I would when older go and fetch medicines from him for home; and when preparing prescriptions for my parents or any of the family, he would raise his shiny bald head and show a red bespectacled humorous face above the separating screen, making wry comments about my father and his involvement in politics, for they were both public workers. The doctor was a very industrious man, who for a hobby had two factories, one a foundry, and the other for making razor blades, thereby becoming relatively wealthy. What endeared 'Old Fletcher' to many people was that he would lavish his skill on rich and poor alike, and if he went to a house where he knew there was genuine poverty, and while attending to his patient was reminded that previous bills had not been settled, he would ask for them and throw them on their fire, forgotten.

There are two other notable characters, one a blind man, and the other a retired headmistress, each individualists. Alan Longden is a physiotherapist, became totally blind while attending the grammar school. Dauntless, he trained for the work he now does in Chesterfield Hospital. Having done the six-mile journeys to and from work daily by bus, one day he decided for a change he'd walk home! It would be over twenty years since he had seen his route, yet at only one place did he ask to be put right. As for his wife, hearing of his escapade she was justifiably alarmed, but like others of us, very proud of his resolution.

Perhaps no one has more influence upon a district than head teachers, one of whom is still keenly alive to happenings in the locality, though retired. Miss Lydia Village is a great Christian who practises her beliefs, and who in her professional days ensured all her pupils were cared for spiritually as well as academically. Occasionally, when addressing habitually late pupils, who through laziness were unpunctual, she would say, "Now my dears, you are late again, this will never do! Do you realize our Heavenly Father has not heard your voices praising Him from the Assembly? It must grieve Him that you attach no importance to this matter. You must do something to rectify this state of affairs; it is sinful to be lazy, and your laziness is deplorable, for it is becoming a habit, and habits are not easily broken. Now, you must each do something immediately to prevent the habit getting hold upon you. How can I put before employers your names for worthwhile jobs, if you cannot make the effort to be there when he should expect you? In the morning I shall be in assembly, and will expect you there to begin our morning praises; now go, and consider what has been said to you." Her kind eyes would glisten with some admonition, yet not enough to embitter them; and Lydia Village has many folk who greatly respect her for her character-building in their formative years.

After only four days at home to attend the ruby wedding, and other functions, I was off on 25 October 1971—leaving the sound of Dronfield's church clock and the clanging power hammers—by the open fields to Unstone. Gone was the once huge colliery spoil-heap which under a reclamation scheme has made the once ugly blotch disappear and reveal a beautiful village again. At the location of one-time back-to-back miners' houses, there are now pleasant semi-detached dwellings with beautiful lawns and flowers. As if to stimulate interest in horticulture in the area is a Len Adlington whose superb topiary work is only equalled by that of experts in mansion grounds. His giant peacock could almost strut amongst the other beautifully shaped privets, and must stir up some secret envy in the minds of others with less experience.

I would not have the time to go by Whittington's Revolution House where King James's overthrow was plotted, and instead went through Brushes, where there is a sign indicating it is the centre of industrial England. A dull, leaden sky did not reveal Chesterfield's crooked spired church in all its glory; nevertheless, the still twisted and alarmingly leaning pyramid continued to defy all forces which would threaten its downfall. Old folks believed the devil got his tail wrapped around it, and in his violent hurry caused a near calamity. It is obviously due to insufficiently seasoned timbers drying out rapidly under the heated leadwork, on the sunniest aspect of the south-west, and creating a lean in that direction of about seven feet.

Chesterfield's greatest pride is in being the resting place of George Stevenson, the great railway engineer. Where he lived at Tapton House (now a school), he used to delight in playing with his grandchildren, and having them race to see who could get up the steep lawns to the top first.

I left this busy engineering place, and one of the most beautiful cricket grounds in England, into the county's fields of inherent wealth of black diamonds—coal.

It seemed pitiable to be walking down the eastern rather than the western side of Derbyshire. My route would take me through the colliery areas, yet the other would have been through hill country, limestone gorges, lush pasture and agricultural lands, and superb river meadows, with a few exciting towns and villages to wander around. I missed Haddon and Chatsworth and kept my nose south-eastwards towards Dover, and having left the washdays of Chesterfield behind I was within the half hour at 'Gressmoor', pardon—Grassmoor. The huge pit bank had been bulldozed and is now the intermittent venue of traction engine rallies; then, up and down the lollopping whippets of colliers could be seen while their masters were strolling around the old, disused pit districts.

Still, some older types of dirty, soot-begrimed houses stood not far away; but nearto, at Williamthorpe, the pleasant semi-detached dwellings occupied this area, smiled upon from the high plateau of Bolsover and its castle. Here, miners still sit around on their haunches when chatting, a natural position like that adopted in the mines when 'grubbing up', instead of sitting in the wet muck. I asked one ageing man what he had done in his working years, and without saying what, he moved his stick vertically in an up and down motion, adding, "Fifty years; I'd had enough."

Reg Goddard, a retired miner who showed me his Fearneough decoration for saving life as an underground ambulance worker, discussed mining with me, since my father once owned a small one. Reg had worked in Grassmoor, where in such a district in the old days, the pit was the only place where boys could get work. Some lads would continue all their working life getting coal, others of a more able type would go for evening school training and become deputies, responsible for the safety in mines, avoiding roof falls and explosions. The top boys could even reach managerial positions and it is always heartening to men trapped below when they know the manager has worked his way through the colliery, and has the courage to go down if need be to offer help.

There have always been big demands regarding the health of miners and particularly in the former times when wet conditions would cause pneumonia, consumption and rheumatism; today with mechanization and dust, respiratory troubles make the occupation a difficult way of making a living. We both remembered the 'Paddy Mail', the colliers' train, coming into Dronfield, returning miners home, which on a number of occasions, on being shunted into the sidings to remain overnight, contained men asleep through weariness so intense they did not waken to alight at their home station. Only the hard wooden seats and glassless windows revived them sufficiently to make them aware of their location.

We spoke of Grassmoor's explosion and its sorry toll of lives, and Duckmanton worse still and finally even in modern times, Creswell, where eighty men were lost through a conveyor belt becoming ignited through friction and poisoning the victims with noxious fumes.

For relaxation some men become expert bandsmen, competing for the greatest trophies at Bellevue and London.

It is most grim 'underneath', such a life causes some to have serious lung troubles, severe rheumatism and worst of all blindness. There is no wonder men clamour for the highest wages of any industry, in order to prepare for an earlier retirement. If anyone begrudging their demanding attitude, we agreed the claimants could take on the job themselves—the first step being on to the quivering cage, and hearing the safety gate go 'click'!

Before the great collieries flourished, indicative of prosperity by the gigantic proportions of their spoil-heaps, there were some superb situations for beautiful halls and manor houses. Fortunately some heaps are being bulldozed into great hollows and given soil coverings, thereby reclaiming lands lost under the spoils. There are some being grassed over in areas which may someday give pasturage, or yet be turned into woodland, with trees that can be supported by providing an anchorage of good soil to start them growing. Who knows, with serious attempts at conservation, these industrial scars may become areas of beautiful landscape.

Less than two miles away, I passed Sutton Scarsdale Hall, and the renowned Hardwick Hall dominating a great scene west and north. The first hall is now a majestic ivyclad ruin, looking down with its great façade of fluted columns and pediment upon the roaring track of the M1. It is a sublime ruin of finely bolstered ashlar and carved Corinthian columns, which would draw many more visitors to see its noble profile had it been in the east. The snows of winter pencil each arris and cornice gracefully, and in summer a floral façade and defence of stinging nettles and prickling thistles debar a closer look into its secrets.

This hall had formerly housed the Earls of Scarsdale and latterly become the residence of the Arkwrights of cotton spinning fame, hence by reason of their great wealth much superb skilled craftsmanship embellished both the exterior and interior of their mansion. After the illustrious family successors left, less interest attended the place, needing obvious periodic attention; thus it lapsed into its present ruined condition, morbidly accepting a doleful future.

Here I was joined and escorted by my two friends Roger Redfern and Frank Hepworth. We three together progressed along the typical Derbyshire byroad, between the low hawthorn hedges, with here and there aged deciduous trees setting the boundaries of farmlands, and we were able to see across the valley to Hardwick Hall. Today's dull weather did not enhance the beauty of such a noble and massive structure, now, for a long time, being in its 'strait-jacket' of steel scaffolding, for repairs on such mansions seem endless. What a fine view does this building command, even today, with an odd whiff of steam and smoke away in the industrial distance. Bess of Hardwick picked a fine site for her palace, which sweeps down a hundred feet of grassy slopes and coppices; still a paradise. She had this hall built 'more glass than wall' with a fine view from every window, yet still with a formidable appearance to any foe, for its boundary walls are surrounded at intervals with decorative stone pikes, all seeming threats to any intruders.

For embellishment the mansion has a great roof-level balustrade, interspaced with a huge frieze of beautifully worked stone including at intervals over each bay Elizabeth of Hardwick's initials E.S. (Elizabeth of Shrewsbury). She was an obvious extrovert, for most architects designed initials in the solid, emblazoning escutcheons seen only in relief of shadow. Not Bess; her initials are seen starkly from below, against the sky, clear cut, choose what the weather, indicating "This can be seen to be mine, that of Elizabeth of Shrewsbury."

By the time we had said about all we knew of Hardwick, Haddon, Chatsworth and Sutton, together with lesser-known gems of historic buildings in Derbyshire, we were out of the county into Nottinghamshire, the highest part of Sutton-in-Ashfield, where my friends returned homewards after seeing me safely with the Meakins, where I was well cared for.

26 *Farms and Pheasants*

It was difficult to believe that this peaceful place of clean brick buildings and pleasant market place had known a turbulent history. Before the time when Queen Victoria's silk hosiery was made there, and later sovereigns had their socks produced on its renowned knitting machines, there had been early in the nineteenth century poor workers who eked a living from using hand machines, who feared loss of work when powered ones were introduced. Some were probably amongst the Luddite members who, masked, entered factories on dark nights and destroyed equipment that they feared would rob them of their livelihood. So serious were their designs on destruction, they continued under threat of death penalties, but now it is different, as the town is renowned for its knitting products.

Sutton's history is coloured by the characters who have lived in, or passed through, it, like the unhappy Cardinal Wolsey who in disgrace was returning to London a sick man. When near the town he could scarcely ride his mule, and by the time he reached Leicester Cathedral, his last ride was 'shoulder high', for he died there in 1530. If only the man had been in happier circumstances riding along through the great Sherwood Forest, he may well have seen stags and hinds in the misty glades before coming into the village and undoubtedly also viewed the best scenery in Nottinghamshire.

A local clergyman, so distressed by conditions of the poor, invented a hand knitting machine to turn out more work to provide knitters with a better livelihood.

A former magistrate was fined a farthing for having a respectable person's home searched without warrant, and rather than indicate guilt by paying the fine, went bankrupt for £30,000.

A new start took me through the market and soon by huge fields passing the gaunt skeleton of an old tramcar single decker in a little croft. I knew then I was on the 'right lines' and gladly traipsed through the woodland bracken to Newstead Priory. This day it was all forlorn except for folk prepared to defy the boisterous wind, and as I sat in the shelter waiting for eventualities of a colour shot, Mrs Daft and her relative sat and talked with me, a rare enjoyment between my halts of morning and evening.

We discussed poor Byron, who used to go from here on horseback to visit friends, for he had many enemies—gossips, with nothing better to do. No wonder he travelled widely to get out of it. How tragic, that lameness should go twinned with such a noble face and brilliant mind, bringing such loneliness to the man as he went about. Yet here in the heart of Nottinghamshire he was able to wander with his dog, unblamed, respected and worshipped; and yet again, I had wandered round to his dog's grave to read the poem written by its master and recorded on the tomb.

Leaving Newstead, I had a lonely tramp through Long Dale and Oxton Bogs scarcely seeing anyone for six miles. Playful peewits tumbled erratically about the sky, swooping in unpredictable paths until weary, and gently settling amidst the corn stubble, scare able to be seen a few yards away, when another company would take the air for like activity. What lovelier bird takes flight than a good cock pheasant with such a gorgeous waistcoat of colour, shapely head and unique tail? Nottinghamshire seemed to me before I left it to have the finest colonies of pheasants and peewits in the kingdom, and thankfully none of these folk with cocked guns who are termed sportsmen.

Reaching Oxton, the time when men were cycling home from work, I asked one the direction for Southwell. "Yes, you're right for Suth'l, round here, and up the hill," and off he trundled.

The old stone church with its reference to the great feat of a national hero thrilled me, for Frank Hepworth used to play against the Oxton cricket team when the late captain St Vincent Sherbrooke V.C. would attend the game. The great man, while serving in the *Onslow* in the Second World War, lost an eye while defending a convoy going to North Russia in 1942.

The evening light gave added warmth to the red-brick cottages and barns, with their gaping vent-holes, while large trees and a fine large house, north of the church, added that distinctive touch of one village differing from another. Further, Oxton can boast connection with the Kennedys of America: and what time I had in it, and saw, taking it unawares, it would be ready any time for a queen's visitation.

Just before leaving to do the last four hectic, heavy miles, I chanced to see the fellow who had directed me standing at his doorway. Our gazes met: I nodded "Good evening", when he replied, "You'll be glad to get a cup o' tea when you get to Suth'l!"

"Yes I will!" and felt a little more creative thinking on his part would have eased the situation before reaching my 'digs'. I'm sure a heavy journey is more memorable, as I found this to be. It is beautiful country steeply undulating, clean away from industry's sprawl, a place for Rowland Hilder; grand fields and hedgerows sweeping down and up again, great sledging country for farm lads when the winter's work day's done.

Then scrambling up 200 feet, the distant landscape ridge with its farm and neighbouring trees surmounted by a crescent moon looked like a caravan of eastern merchants over the desert of darkening land and as I walked they were gone—asleep perhaps, for no calling dog, or owl, or any mortal thing made the slightest sound. For company, the moon, though very young, tried hard to brighten my route, but it was no use; it would have been magnificent to see the landscape in the daylight, but on I plodded underneath dark trees scarcely seeing the road but for the lights of very few cars. Night-time is the occasion of many thoughts, and not a few on this were of a place thirty miles north-west; but soon I was resting my weary limbs in an inn. Opposite was the Saracen's Head, where Charles I laid his head in 1642, maybe sleepless with troubles. Myself, I went off like a log!

Scrutinizing my map as to the day's journey, and feeling like nothing on earth, for a shocking cold had developed, I chose Bingham—never even heard of it, but at least it was south-east. I couldn't risk more than the ten miles or I would be 'out on a limb'. This shorter journey gave me time to spare, to look round the magnificent Southwell Minster with its severe twin-towered west face. I am never excited about the outside, but once inside the door, my elation is beyond bounds, in fact my normal procedure of saving the best features to scrutinize until last goes by the board, for the building is full of superlative wonders.

To start with, if it is sunny, and shafts of light through the clerestory windows impinge on the great Norman columns, it is fascinating to watch the poetic beauty of the changing shapes of light and shadow on the red stones that seem to be built for eternity. Next to stand near the altar and look down the building is a moving sight; and worth more than a glance at the sculptured figure of the kneeling bishop.

The next *must* be seen: to visit Southwell without seeing the 'Leaves of Southwell' would be dire indeed. They are world-famous column bosses in the chapter house, wrought with incredible skill in fragile stone, to represent the leaves found in Sherwood Forest. The foliage is intertwined with the spacings pierced and undercut, and even ribbed in some places where not normally seen. The sculptor of mediaeval times is unknown, but whose skill, unsurpassed in one medium, induced woodcarvers to produce equally magnificent productions in wood showing foliage, fruit and birds. There is no place anywhere that I have seen with wood so finely fashioned. It would appear, on looking around the choir stalls, that a dozen Grinling Gibbons had been at work.

I went outside into the fierce light an hour and a half later to make up for time I should have been walking, and ambled towards Halloughton. There is only Tideswell church in the Peak District which thrills me like unto the view of Southwell Minster as I looked back to the sunlit town, to see it standing amongst the leafless trees, ready for winter's sleep. There was a clean, windswept appearance of the land and hedgerows as I passed Nottinghamshire's Agricultural College which seemed inordinately quiet. Perhaps the students were in Southwell, taking graftings from Bramley's seedling apple tree, now so old that the trunk's weighty bulge has taken root where it touches the ground. I was determined to make some progress when before me was one of those scenes like finding the Cullinan diamond amongst all the gems of the empire. It was a pleasant autumn morning, with tidy fields and a little lane branching off to a hamlet; from the lane a large, dark hew hedge fenced the churchyard, with the little open belfried building standing silhouetted in the light, as a grazing herd of Charolais cattle lay or stood about contented, completing a picture the epitome of the English countryside—and here I recorded my best scenic picture.

Continuing in weakness I ambled by pastures and undulating ploughed lands to Thurgarton, a village where children can play without all the mechanical contrivances to make them happy. It is a dream village in a million, with little offshoot lanes, charming cottages, and a little stream, and contains a queer-looking clock on a stand, much like a Mad Hatter's watch of giant size; and barns with vent-holes through which imaginary fiends spy ready to shoot at 'comers' into the locality. I never would get on at this rate snooping around, for Boot's chemists have a research place in an old fine hall, near the magnificent priory. The priory was once almost equal in size with Southwell Minster, with indications of great splendour, and still there is something awe-inspiring about Thorgeirr—Norse—of great antiquity, yet as I went round the old edifice, where shaling stone had fallen in little heaps by the massive doorway arch, these gave practical proof of decay and the need for vigilant care and maintenance.

My legs wouldn't go as my journey led to Lowdham, another village with a pleasant stream and better-class houses; probably many occupants have yachts or boats on the nearby Trent at Gunthorpe bridge, for some folk were out idly riding on the river, blue as the Mediterranean in their colourful craft.

My thirst on this idle day of heavy cold and shaky knees was such I called in a 'local'—householders don't want the bother of every Tom and Dick calling for liquid refreshment. However, the visitors were plenty and well engaged in 'bending the elbow' while chatting about this and that, when another subject developed upon my arrival. Someone asked me, "What are you up to?" Before leaving the whole company to continue with their solving of Britain's problems, I asked for something of interest about Lowdham, which unanimously revolved around a pleasant fellow who gave me his story, which was vouched for by the honest publican and his wife to be the truth about Dennis Plumb's brush with the law.

Mr Dennis Plumb, while walking through fields in the locality, observed watercress growing in a fresh waterbed, owned by a Commander and squire of the village. However, Dennis may not have been aware he was trespassing and acquired some watercress, being observed by the squire doing so, who commanded him to get in his car with the cress, to be taken to the police sergeant. The officer then took the offender to the railway station to have the vegetation weighed, and, asked if he was satisfied with the weight indicated on the scale, he remarked "You've weighed the water an' all!" The sergeant replied, "You've pinched——water also, ain't yer?" Accused was fined £2. Folk became aware of this amount, which a friend told his wife he had paid, unbeknown to Dennis; and going to the local pub, his acquaintances, commiserating with the offender 'clubbed up' yielding £1 10s. 0d., so he was that amount financially better off for having stolen the cress.

Crossing the Trent, the magnificence at the top of the wooded rise could only be better in the pilot's cockpit high above the aerodrome. 'Standing to stare', I then crossed over Foss Way, near Newton, and finally 'docked' in Bingham at the Chesterfield Arms run admirably by the publican Len Sparrow and his German wife.

Thankfully my visual torpor and general lack of energy improved after a bath, when I felt a little better and was about to stroll out into the twilight pending a late meal and slung my camera on my shoulder. The reason being, I was charmed by the old market square and its butter cross and felt a shot showing it lit up would look nice. Mr Sparrow saw me and expressed surprise that I should attempt photography when it was going dark, yet it proved one of my nicest shots.

Whilst snooping around outside the dimly-lit church and its lychgate, I heard an organ playing and so stole inside to look at the interesting features under the conditions of night-time. The beautiful altar of boldly carved wood showed the figures of Christ, and the patron saint of a Bingham family. These figures however were different, for they were smiling, an attitude to life which seemed to be reflected in the faces of the local people.

My dinner would be ready in an hour; but by the time I'd sauntered round the church listening to the caretaker and her son, the time had flown, having to make a dash to the Chesterfield Arms to keep my appointment.

About the church it was apparent the carvers of one generation and another had had a heyday in their time, both old and young, for carvings on a fascia showed some of the things used in our Lord's passion such as the different tools—the hammer and pincers, the dice and whips. Then symbolic of a saint's protection of small children, there hung over the font the splendid effigy of St George slaying the dragon; and yet another 18-inch carving of a grand old woman carrying her basket stood in prominence, the story being that old Ann Harrison who lived to over ninety had made a habit of collecting odds and ends from villagers and making useful things from them. Whenever she had collected two half-crowns from sales of the goods, these were given for the work of the church, having made good use of her time by industry and cheerful visitations in the parish.

Queer markings on the wall in the side chapel, which were made by the school pupils who formerly used the church for lessons, were formed by the sharpening of slate pencils, some indeed beautiful, since queer little faces were etched out indicative of happy lessons.

It was 7.30 when I hurried off to sit at a welcome table and thereafter make my log; and bed.

I breakfasted like a monarch and asked for my bill, but the landlord munificently ignored my question and thus I left Len Sparrow's household happy as a lark, and 'flew' off towards Melton Mowbray, even though I was still out of form, and was soon amongst tremendous fields of sprouting winter wheat—heading for Leicestershire.

On my way, some folk asked me, "What do you think about on your long lonely stretches?"

I've thought of the many kindnesses that have happened to me throughout my life and thanked God for the beautiful things tucked away in city, town, village and hamlet; while enriching my life with the philosophies of ordinary and extraordinary people.

In this outpost of Nottinghamshire the greatest drive of intensive farming appeared; mechanical ditching had drained the great tracts of land, and wooden fences set boundaries to respective farms. The wooden posts and rails had a certain attractive appearance in their long rows of perspective, so different from Scotland's posts and wire fences, or the walls of Yorkshire and hedgerows of Derbyshire. There was one aspect of farming these boundaries did not limit—the 'ripe' odours of manure from the working spreader, and I'm glad there was a mutual sharing between myself, the potato gatherers and the fellows delving huge craters with bull-dozers.

Farmers were ripping out thick hedges and burning the whole lot in tremendous fires, and in the craters giant tree roots which would not burn or easily decay were being dragged into them and covered by earth and topsoil. This mechanically cleared area, which will soon be covered with corn or other crops, will be the great frontage to the castle-like Winnerton Hall, the former gate-house to the original castle Cromwell destroyed. This beautiful mansion is owned by Major-General Sir Miles Graham, formerly understudy to General Montgomery.

The picture of the English landscape is changing, the once beautiful hedges of hazel, hawthorn and holly, the habitats of birds, hedgehogs, and rodents, are now being replaced by soulless wood and wire, or infantry troops of posts and rails, to ensure less shadows fall on crops which do not dry out so well near sheltering hedges.

Next, passing through little Harby famous for its cheeses and seeing the huge wartime nearby aerodrome, I was soon on Scalford, with its Snowcemmed cottages with pantiled roofs. Dominating this village was a square-towered church, mellowed, in amongst the trees, with a unique porch containing the still very evidently bloodstained flagstones where a Roundhead was murdered. I enjoyed Nottinghamshire and could well have settled hereabouts, but made progress again amidst mixed farmlands supporting a few fine horses now into the county of Leicestershire.

Distant trees and farmsteads began to be enshrouded in cottonwool mistiness when nearby there appeared a curious factory chimney attached to a farmstead, which proved to have a corn grinding mill formerly driven by steam from a boiler, which needed a good draught for its fire. The corn when ground digests better and is more beneficial to the beasts. Curiously enough I saw no pigs, which are used to provide meat for products from Melton Mowbray I was now entering.

Reaching the town, I was fortunate in seeing the magnificent St Mary's church in all its glory after the end of its 800th anniversary celebrations. Much care must have been lavished on its cleaning, as I have never before seen such clean stone, wood and glass. Having wandered round in the evening, seeing the massive tower under the effect of spot-lighting, my decision for next morning was to spend all my allocation of viewing time on seeing the church.

A daring special feature of the construction is in having an enclosed stair added to one corner of the tower, which being so carefully designed doesn't destroy the balance of the structure. Inside the building, one feels mortal insignificance on seeing the colossal size of the Gothic pillars, and standing beneath the stretching limbs of the arches, one's attention is focused on the glorious glass of the fine windows, which give a mellow light due to the various rich colours used. But whereas in many sanctuaries the interest is mainly in geometrical shapes, here in Melton Mowbray's masterpiece the glass preaches sermons or records of history. Some glass refers to the Christian martyrs, the rest to the miracles and parables of Christ. There is one fault; I'm afraid if I sat listening to the greatest oration from the pulpit and my eyes wandered even momentarily to the windows, my ears would go deaf, but the east window with its fifteen panels gave me my greatest thrill in the art of the ecclesiastical glazer.

Viewing time gone, I tore myself away with what feeble

energy I could muster and shuffled towards Oakham, knowing Roger Redfern on his mid-term holiday would be coming to stroll with me. Undeterred by dreadful fog, Roger made me aware of his presence by a cheerful "Good morning" as his car drew up behind me. But for him, my target would have been Oakham, where the old castle walls are decorated with horse-shoes which were once paid as tolls by visiting peers to Rutland. My friend, by relays, kept me company, as I went by dwellings beautifully roofed with decorative thatch and where at Langham a lady showed us through her property all set for 5 November, with a long hose-pipe to prevent the thatch firing from any stray rockets.

Next followed the most hauntingly beautiful county of this realm with the road undulating and swaying, following the contours of the land. It seemed as if the monotonous, dull, routine jobs of industry were more than a million miles away, and that clangs and clatters of hammers were only to be found in Vulcan's forge and that all mythological. We had detoured when in 6½ miles there would not be six vehicles pass us and one of those an intruding tractor. Quaint old cottages and halls and cooing doves; vast wide verges for pasturing ponies or gorging goats seemed everywhere, but nothing of this mad world in a hurry.

Roger had taken his car for the last relay into Uppingham when an old man with his grand-daughter and dog accompanied me a while, who said everyone seems in happy relationship in those parts. Take for instance the fine farmer Marshall Turner, who in former times used to care for old people and gave all his workmen 'Christmas time come' a large piece of beef and a big plate-size mince pie. He got the best out of his men; and if he were alive now, there would be men who would still do the same good service in return.

It seemed amazing; by the time the party of three turned back to the distant cottages, I had barely two miles to go, for with Roger's company the journey had been shortened, and soon we were at Miss Lowe's home in Uppingham having an excellent Derbyshire meal, giving him a good start for his return journey home.

27 *Spires and Squires*

After an old-fashioned remedy the dear old lady gave me at the A.A. hotel, I had slept like a top, much abler to journey to Kettering, and out into a shocking fog. I peered at what buildings I was able to locate. The fine buildings and courtyard of the Uppingham sixteenth-century school are a delight and not less the quaint church and superb ancient cottages. Here is epitomized the skill of dedicated former architects, for whom, whether they were designing a cathedral or a cottage, the same principles held, viz: fitness for use, elegance and economy. I'll call again on a sunny day.

On we groped, that is, crawling traffic—and myself even faster—for as I left 'something' Lazars, long queues of traffic were halted by a huge flock of sheep in the road. I never saw such chaos. Dogs with half-cocked ears and drooping tails awaiting commands, shouting shepherds, muttering motorists —I was fortunate to be able to proceed.

I had not asked the swarthy man for directions from 'something' Lazars, I should have missed my way, for his speech was strong and mellow with 'glass' like *glarrsss*. He wished me well into the *forrrg* when ultimately I unearthed Caldecott. Here in the village public house I ordered coffee, as the sign indicated 'Coffee now being served'.

"Sorry, we can't serve coffee this morning."

"Well sir, it says coffee is now being served."

"Where?"

"On your notice board."

"Where is the board?"

"In your porch entrance."

"Oh, if t'board's outside, coffee is on; if it's inside, it's off."

I argued no more, had something else and felt tempted to reverse the board as I left.

As soon as the county boundary was crossed, the power of the sun transformed the landscape, as if the proscenium lights had come to replace the curtain gloom of fog. Never had I seen such a miraculous change and never a prettier village on my route in England. I had reached Rockingham, a place where foreigners must dote upon. I was so thrilled I wanted to anchor myself all day to sit and draw—perhaps another time.

I waited an age for someone to provide life in my photograph of the village cross in the long steep street, and eventually was rewarded. The old stone houses with trim, wide, grass verges seemed to have grown out of the steep hillside and smiled over the gorgeous Welland Valley. Higher up the road, both the church and castle stood dominantly, and must have originally given strong senses of protection and blessing on the inhabitants; and one must agree that Dickens chose wisely in making the stronghold a place for his writings.

My pack weighed heavily by the time the vast ironstone plateau of Corby was reached, where tremendous changes have taken place in the last forty years. Many of the folk working in the steel works have travelled south, and one can be excused for thinking oneself in Scotland when in amongst the workers. From now on into Kettering, the landscape seemed scarred and torn in many places, where the rapacious quarrying machines had removed millions of tons of ore. Fortunately nature seems to have reacted with vigour to heal the wounds, by profusely supplying birches, bracken, grass, and scrub which are pleasanter to look upon than tremendous earthy rifts.

Soon the quarried land gave way to fields and woodland, pleasant houses, and thronging crowds on a Saturday afternoon in Kettering, where Tom and Vera Preston gave me a grand homely welcome for a stay of two nights, to offset the 'flu'.

Kettering has long been famous for its shoe industry, and its world-famous brass band; furthermore equipment for children's playgrounds goes to many countries also, the factory owner prospering enough for him to give Kettering its noted Wicksteed Park.

Before continuing, I was taken to see the fantastic mechanical shovel at Corby which could scoop up a bus; to my engineering inclinations it seemed to be the ultimate in man's inventiveness to avoid soul-destroying drudgery.

Next came Eleanor's Cross at Geddington, a superb tribute that Edward I erected in 1290, showing that her bier rested there on its way from Harby to London. The best was yet to be: I was already excited about the magnificence of every Northamptonshire church we passed, for all differed in various architectural features, but especially in spire design, slender and ornate and visible for miles around, gracefully protruding above all the other buildings. There is nowhere in the kingdom with such glorious structures, for the stones seem alive where they form graceful and strong flying buttresses, supporting the high walls of the tallest and most beautiful edifices. We arrived at a smaller church, in Warkton, to see the renowned sculptures, said to be unequalled in any other English church. One which held my greatest attention is the group designed by Robert Adam and worked by P. M. Van Gelder, a feast for any craftsman's eyes. It is said the material was brought to the vicinity so that completed units would not be broken in transit. I am glad I stayed the extra day, to see these examples of the highest skill of the engineer and sculptor found in Northamptonshire. Incidentally, Dr Scholl made a commercially viable sandal by gaining an idea from one depicted on one of the figures of the groups. After our jaunt, Tom Preston, a brilliant trombonist in the band, gave a magnificent demonstration of versatility, and his relative Len Shipley told tales of horses from proud stallions and nags to clothes-horses. Len said how foolish it is for folk to leave field gates open: once, his employer had been stocking some outbuildings with corn for feeding his five fine draught horses, when someone, having passed through the field, left the gate open, allowing the animals to gorge—to death.

With the grand attention given me, and being now on form, I was spurred off towards a mysterious Poddington where immediately out of Kettering were some ancient earthworks much like a former castle moat, followed by Burton Latimer, where even today one could not be surprised at a crinolined lady walking out of the church gate. As I was entering St Mary the Virgin, a woman returned and showed me round as capably as any experienced conductor in a cathedral. She revealed architecture of two different ages both Norman and Gothic, then the carvings of the reredos showing the Lamb of God and angels with censors. Then followed the tale of how the twelve murals are being restored professionally, much to her delight. It was her church and she was full of great enthusiasm about it. I only wish more folk cared like her, for in my time I have seen superb carvings broken, though unintentionally, by being mishandled by inexperienced cleaners.

Leaving Burton Latimer on an open road with bare fields, there assailed my nostrils the smell of tanning leather: but worse things than that have been in these parts of Rothwell and Finedon, for the former is remembered by a great find of hundreds of skulls in a vault, no one knowing why they were there, and to be ever reminded of this gruesome find, the Rothwell football team is known as the 'Bones Club'. Finedon too has had soccer troubles, for close to where I was lunching seated on a wall, my informant said that while a match was in progress some years ago part of the football pitch collapsed into some underground ironstone workings, but fortunately without injury to players.

What Northamptonshire lacks in scenic splendour, it possesses in ecclesiastical wonders: it is a paradise for the connoisseur. Luckily a magnificent spire stood high on a strong rise of land, drawing my attention away from the obnoxious odours from a tanning factory. It dominated Higham Ferrers, which in itself is worthy of a halt; but no finer church of its size have I ever seen including the continent. The church is built of mellowed stone, with graceful high walls and 'living' flying buttresses: arches and traceries beggar description, for mullions, bars, and transomes, while besides satisfying their functions of usefulness, are of exquisite beauty also. Inside is as magnificent as the exterior, the brasses being world-famous. The old cross, also, is as exquisite as the church, and for certain these finds at Higham Ferrers were amongst the greatest treasures found on the journey.

Tearing myself away I flew on through 'hock and dough',

the name given to Wellingborough's famous dish (like Lancashire's tripe and onions), and turned off westwards down a country lane to be accompanied by a retired bachelor for escort.

Here were well-tended fields and hedges and distant coppices which formed the landscape as far as we could see and dusk coming on: but my acquaintance pressed on to tell me how Higham Ferrers church was built, by using soil ramps. It is fascinating that the skilled craftsman could work safely on banking provided by the village labourer, who, when another corner of the building needed constructing, would remove the soil from the completed part to the other site. The supporting soil would then allow the masons to put the finishing strokes to fitted stones.

The time had flown, when Poddington church showed above the trees, as we neared the home croft of the first farm, where some colossal Large White sows and a monstrous boar rummaged and grunted as their noses briskly turned the grass sods. Luckily the farmer was pleasanter than his animals, including the bristling dog, as he told us where Church Farm was; and finding a shop-cum-post office for a few oddments, I then saw my friend off.

My approach to the farmhouse was through the churchyard by an arched doorway, then across by a walled area which keeps animals from the house door, where I knocked firmly and politely. I had a feeling these folk have more to do than wanting my intrusion at this hour, when a lady came. She was old enough to be a grandmother but still young, hardworking, and uncomplaining, glad to see you, even when one comes at awkward times.

If Waterston's farm was anything it was practical, and the meal put on the table the moment Sally came in from school. There is no woman more efficient than an experienced farmer's wife, for besides doing her chores of cleaning, cooking, washing, mending, tending sick folk and maybe caring for a cade lamb, she may have for a hobby the rearing of poultry; she's never still. Mrs Waterston is such a woman who saw to everything I needed later, but for the moment, introduced me to her husband, a typical south Scottish farmer, stocky, fresh-faced, tanned by wind and weather, who spoke in the crisp sentences of the man who makes up his mind and says what he means.

After the meal, Archie Waterston went and made up his farm diary and then invited me to his office, a small room, where on one wall a large map showed the layout of fields and coppices, and the railway alongside his boundary. He was then able at any time to show his land-owner any current or future scheme relating to any part on the farm. His wife and Sally finished off the chores and the latter her homework also, while we men resorted to the best room to discuss procedure in the running of Church Farm.

In 1951 Archie Waterston answered an advertisement for a farm manager, and was invited by a wealthy London businessman to look at the farm.

"What do you think about it?" asked the owner.

"It's in very poor shape, and will need a few years before we see some good returns for labour and outlay," replied the prospective farmer.

"Well, if you think you can put it in the condition that I would like to see it, you can have the job."

"Thank you, I would like to accept the job, and will do my best."

"All right, I will tell you what I want doing first, and then you can tell me what capital you will require to undertake the work," said the employer.

The first morning Archie Waterston told one of his men to walk round the farmyard and buildings with him, and while on the itinerary, the farm man lit a cigarette and threw the empty packet to the ground. The manager said, "Sorry young man, I hope you don't mind, but pick it up, good chap." The whole place needed a tremendous effort to tidy it up, since the yard was filthy with oddments, buildings, doors and gates in disrepair, hedges unkempt and spreading over the land, and a lack of system everywhere.

Next morning the round began again, the same man adopting the same procedure with his 'lighting up', the packet being thrown into the same corner as before.

"I'm sorry, young man, hope you don't mind——"

"I'm sorry Mr Waterston, I forgot myself," said the man as he retrieved the packet, which was the last thrown down;

and mysteriously all other packets and rubbish disappeared from the yard, which took on a new look which it has never lost.

Archie Waterston, the manager, was beginning to be known in the village, when he was told by a local person that he hoped he would last longer than most of his predecessors. Again, from another quarter he heard a similar suggestion but gave it no heed, and continued systematically to get the whole place tidied up, and men to work in teams; ploughing and harrowing for one team, cattle men another, throughout the whole farm.

It was not long before the men doing their own specific jobs grew more efficient, knowing what their work would be on succeeding days, and soon began to take on a responsible pride in their tasks.

Eventually cattle reared on the farm began to win more prizes when exhibited at shows, which gave the herdsmen extra incentive to care for their stock; and therefore all round, the manager and men began to work not as individuals, but as a team determined to make a great success out of combined efforts.

Out of the developing success a respect grew for the manager, and men would settle down to a permanent job on the farm. However, one night a test case arose out of a serious incident. It was lambing time when one young man was in charge of the ewes, for which he had made a good stock pen out of straw bales in the shape of a square, so that the animals would be protected from the chilly winds, while for his own accommodation he had a nearby caravan.

Ewes by nature await the signs of dawn before giving birth, so the young fellow went home about midnight to have supper and say "goodnight" before resuming his work. As he approached his van and opened the door, the whole place broke into flames which were so fierce the straw bales ignited also, into an unmanageable conflagration. He raced to the farm in a state of panic to get help, when Mr Waterston said "Sit down, sit down," to discover what was amiss.

"Fire," was the only word the fellow could say, so the manager phoned the brigade, arranged a cup of tea for the hysterical man, dashed to the field to give help with the fire, and attend to the suffering sheep. The calamity had caused a loss of animals, the straw and the caravan, but the manager, knowing that he had a very conscientious man who had had the misfortune to be involved in an accident, kept him on his staff where he could again regain his confidence in the work. The fire was shown on national TV since an amateur, hearing the fire alarm bell, had snatched up his movie camera and followed the fire engine, making a dramatic record of the disaster. The ultimate outcome of the affair was that a profound respect grew for their master from the workers since he had shown such humanity for his man in time of crisis.

The church farm had now reached an acreage of 1400, since it comprised of the land from various former holdings, and manager and workers now totalling fourteen had made it a showpiece in the county and also the 'pet' of the wealthy owner.

One day owner and manager had been discussing projects when the former said he would like his manager to include further matters in his planning, and putting them to him, the owner mentioned that of the men on the farm, some were married and would retire while still in farm service and while renting a cottage under the holding. The owner stated the obvious that, when a man should retire, he would vacate the cottage for a new workman, *but*, he should not be pitched out into a hostile world, looking round for a place which even he and his wife could not afford in their old age, and the manager was to arrange accommodation for them. He was to keep vigilant for likely property, which could be modified and decorated, and kept dry pending the retirement of a man with his wife, who on the time of maturity could go into the property still near to the farm for which he had worked.

He was also to have a cottage immediately available in case a farm worker should die, leaving a widow; and these newly appointed tasks the manager did with enthusiasm, for it is not every employer or company that is as concerned with the humanitarian as with the commercial side of a business.

We retired, and were up early, which allowed me chance to look at the farmstead and the distant fields, which even in November looked like a 'golden calendar' picture of rural

England at its best. Having walked this far through Britain, I had now seen teamwork at its best which gives both master and men such great satisfaction. When I pass southwards through Wellingborough on the train, my gaze will be fixed on the westward side to see how Archie Waterston and his men are doing, assured that his wife will be on with some good cooking in her cheery kitchen, or maybe for a few moments taking her grandchild for a toddle through the farmyard.

Like the other kindly womenfolk before, my hostess had prepared me the best from her larder, and I was off. At the shop, I was told what a prominent position the folk of Church Farm had in village activities, an especial delight to the community being at Christmas, when Mr Waterston shows his amateur movies of children who get opportunity to see themselves on the screen, showing how they've grown up. The postmaster–shopkeeper shook hands seeing me go, and as I passed between the lovely cottages and network of electric cables, I glanced back at the fine church and watched the vicar who smiled and nodded as he went home surpliced from the morning prayers. He is a thorough parson respected by all, for he is always punctually at church every morning at 7.30, and visits all people in need, and especially unfortunate children in a nearby country hospital. He had just gone when the noise of a chugging tractor heralded the loaded vehicle from Church Farm, which then turned down the lane towards the distant fields, its noise growing less as our separation increased as I turned to go southwards. At last I had seen a happy community in the heart of England, that could work and play together without rancour. "Full many a gem of purest ray serene." Poddington!

The weather was so warm that some Angus calves huddled under a tree out of the strong sunlight, swishing away with their tails, the hundreds of blue-bottles swarming round their eyes and noses, and soon after passing the old mansion hospital conversion, I was in the beautiful curved lanes with pheasants lazily moving through the hedges away from my path. There seemed to be no one for miles when a fellow on a cycle drew level and dismounted to have a chat as he pushed his machine beside me, keeping me splendid company.

Mr Line was seventy-one and daily exercised by cycling, and could be estimated to be sixty-five at most, for, as an extra exercise, he cultivated a sizeable garden. This activity to us was mutual, and kept us chatting about growing peas while avoiding their destruction by birds. His novel way of dealing with rats and mice was, that bare hands must not set traps, or they will be avoided. The 'young' man then reluctantly turned about and left the world to me.

Sometimes in my philosophizing, I wondered why my geography teachers had never really enthused me over the beauty of *my* country. About Switzerland and Austria, about Norway and Sweden, yes, but not about Northamptonshire or Bedfordshire. Away off the main traffic roads free of the squalor of waste paper, packets, and bottles, the 'B' roads and lanes are the streets of Paradise, where hedgerows bloom with stitchwort, red campion, bird's eye, cowherb or cow parsley, buttercups, daisies, foxgloves and ivy, which made me a happy journey into Bedfordshire.

28 *Where Honesty Pays*

GOING through a county by main road or rail gives an incomplete idea of the community life of its villages and hamlets, so I journeyed through several such places possessing beautiful cottages, brick-built with elegant chimneys and freshly painted woodwork and some even roofed in thatch. On I strolled where lorries or juggernauts seemed foreign to the quiet lanes until a hamlet was reached, where bending branches still bore fruit. Gathered apples placed in plastic bags were piled high on a rickety table at the outside corner of an orchard where a notice indicated the price, and for any purchases made the money was to be placed in a basin. A little further on, fruit and vegetables were arranged not unlike a harvest festival or Covent Garden display, again with price indications for each group of produce, with the basin for cash at the side. This showed Ruskinian idealism in practice, which can happen and does, even in the Gorbals of Glasgow. I was thrilled, and more so as I turned into the sleepy village of West End.

Ebbington had another display board that indicated a Baptist chapel, where a former friend of mine preaches. He saw me and showed me round the old place, with its ancient balcony and still working antique clock. Folk around Ebbington directed me off my route to see the street where Bunyan imagined that "Pilgrim's burden fell off his back and rolled into the river and was seen no more." I took a photo of the place, using a 'live' interest in the foreground for which I waited ten minutes and with an itinerant salesman speaking to me I forgot to wind the film on, spoiling two main photographs.

Then on the Hill Shoulder was a fine windmill of National Trust heritage, stark against the sharp light, for which I scrambled around for foreground interest, trespassing more than likely, but folk didn't mind as they dumped their sugar beet and potatoes into large sheds away from the foraging sows.

Kempston, my next accommodation, was still some distance as I passed between giant fields of brussels sprouts 'buttoning up' for market. Two market gardeners welcomed a strange voice as they eased their backs from the monotonous jobs of applying fertilizers near the roots of multitudes of plants, and soon when they are marketable the men will, frozen-fingered, break off each sprout (sprouts like frost) and peel off the outer leaves by the million and put the vegetables in crates and ship them off to Covent Garden.

The mist of evening after a warm day settled low on the wide landscape, while the receding couple looked disembodied with grey plastic aprons round their middles. Some acreage bereft of crops now ploughed showed the silvery sheen of furrows in the waning light as the pale moon slowly rose, and 'stay out late' gnats did their phantom dance near the roadside hedge as I entered the next village passed by scurrying lighted cars from Bedford.

Eventually I was glad to hear the northern voices of Douglas and Mrs Taylor and family settled south, where he is a peripatetic teacher of music in Bedfordshire schools—but what the Dickens it was that caused my lack of sleep, heaven knows, I coughed and coughed all night—dust from ploughing?

After fine hospitality I set out on a tremendous journey, feeling dreadfully weary. Soon, leaving the town, I saw the familiar sight of legions of brick chimneys indicating the colossal brickworks, whose supplies already form the countless brick buildings of London and other cities. As I saw the long graves of worked-out pits, it occurred to me if only those 'poking fingers' which are of no further use were demolished and the pits no longer commercially viable were filled and covered with topsoil, the site would look tidier and provide a yield of crops again.

There were no heralds as I passed through the village of Wilstead, as when William the Conqueror, having called there, ensured the place having a suitable name to commemorate the special occasion, namely Wilhampstead, now briefly Wilstead.

By now, in large expanses of countryside with fields and hedgerows, remotely bounded by coppices, there were to the north, the giant Cardington airship hangars. A few solitary barrage balloons snootily looked down, indicating some current activity of the Air Ministry's concern; but silenced were the roars from their former leviathan airships which once sailed so benignly over the locality. In the 'twenties, designers had strong ambitions for the successful use of these giant craft, which owing to horrifying disasters, were doomed to failure.

By a stroke of good fortune, I came in contact with Mr A. E. Gerrish who, having been the Construction Manager at the Royal Airship Works at Cardington from 1920 onwards, told me with enthusiasm about some of his experiences. He frequently met important visitors, but one, for whom he had to make sure he had a tidy route of inspection, was the late Prince of Wales. Albert Gerrish, ignoring the instruction from high officials, had two workmen strategically placed where the Prince would pass and told them not to move on any account. Thus, when the Royal Personage later had to stride over the workmen, it caused him real amusement and saw proceedings more truly representative of normal working.

Mr Gerrish worked on the ill-fated R101 which was due for a return trip to India in early October 1930, and was highly disappointed, with a number of others, when his name did not appear on the passenger list. He now regards himself as fortunate, for all voyagers perished when the vessel crashed in France at Beauvais. By strange coincidence Mr and Mrs Gerrish came again into my story, but for the present I threshed in sweltering heat unbelievable for November and much against my will detoured four miles to see a village. A load is always heavier, the boots always tighter, and the thirst is always keener, the sweat a bigger nuisance, each mile a good lot longer, when one does a walk unwillingly; but resolution spurred me on. Not a breath stirred, not a man, machine, animal or bird moved one jot in all that panorama, but BANG went the most frightening, shattering crack of my life! Is some fool shooting at me from the hedge? I thought, and rushed forward with all the speed I could, never any

A scene near Southwell

Bingham butter market

Rockingham

A giant shovel at Corby

At Harrold, near Bedford – a masterpiece of mason's art

Old Warden

His only friends – taken in St James's Park, London

The Albert Memorial, London – 'Sharing Pomp'

Dickens' Leather Bottle, at Cobham

Canterbury Cathedral – the ceremony of turning a page in the Book of Remembrance, which takes place daily at 11 a.m.

Near the end!

Dover Castle – at last

faster in all my route. With an eye over my shoulder and careering madly on, looking for the slightest move, I still saw no one when another similar bang went off but this time more distant from the hedge. After a third shot still frighteningly loud the noise seemed from the middle of the large, newly-sown field of possible winter wheat, when my fears were allayed, and later confirmed, by a local cyclist that the 'shots' were from either acetylene or fuse-fired bird scarers. Heavens, farmers of the future, place such contraptions further off a highway, please!

The 'cold water' on my spine being neutralized by my endeavours, the dream village of Old Warden came into view, and beggars my pen to describe it. Why doesn't someone make pictures of these precious spots on earth and record them in volumes for the ardent searcher after beauty to see, and know where to locate them. (Pardon my seeming conceit —perhaps when I've done this treatise there's the job for me.) The whole road is lined with gardens containing cottages that are the antithesis of the modern trend and vie with one another in various riots of charm. Each house differs from any other and is singularly beautiful, and an edifice to be doted upon: its windows are like beautiful eyes beaming welcome, its door a mouth that speaks welcome, its walls a complexion caressed with flowers. Its 'hair' is something to rave about, for who saw fairer thatch in any other place on earth than Old Warden? Each dwelling has a roof of thatch that were it likened to a duchess, it would appear she were to be presented to a queen.

The barge boards, the precious skills of keenest craftsmen, seem like embroidered combs, to contain the 'hair', curved and pierced in grandiose patterns all differing one house from another.

The only permission for anyone to live in this village of the Shuttleworth Estate is to be a worker for the Estate, the crest of which is a shuttle held in hand.

Going the full length of the village to satisfy my curiosity, it was impossible for me to visit the interior of the old church rich in carving, or the light aircraft museum formed as a memorial to the heir of the Shuttleworth Estate who was killed in the war. A lonesome plane droned as it wove a pattern in the duck-egg sky, while a gentleman farmer discussed his crossed breeds herd of cows. Hereford cows crossed with a Friesian bull, he said, give the Hereford bulk of beef and the milk yield of the Friesian.

There was the sharpest light of evening between the great trees in the park of the Agricultural College as I furtively passed the one-time mansion, to shorten my detour, and before the full length of the carriageway had been traversed, cock pheasants idly strutted close by whilst a wary rabbit on his haunches sat, ears cocked, eyeing me at a safe distance from the field border of long grass.

My trespass over, I strove out towards Shefford, under a sky suffused with a glowing sunset, passing innumerable stacked crates of brussels sprouts ready for night despatch for London. As darkness gathered, the green produce of the fields merged with the dun colour of the soil of ploughed and harrowed lands, until all were alike and only for me the nightmare of a pathless road trying to dodge the furious driving of fiendish motorists until I found digs in the nearest village.

Again my luck held, the weather on yet another day was perfect and as soon as practicable I was off through pleasant villages, and where rich autumn tints glowed from the huge sycamores near the old inn at Clifton, unknowingly used my colour camera for the last time—the weather 'broke'. Thereafter the road twisted in and around the peaceful fields spread over with the unbroken sunshine; who would think that in two days' time the sky would be torn with the ragged edges of property parapets and soaring skyscrapers? I made the best of the flying moments and wandered into Norton's old church of St Nicholas and saw not the fine and elegant but the simple and practical, nothing to take one's mind off the devotions. The dark wood of the pews, balustrading, pulpit, and sounding board gleamed with the thoroughness of regular cleaning and the white walls glistened to the very limits of roof trusses and rafters. It was a perfect gem of simple church architecture, recorded by photography because a nearby publican offered to help me with his kitchen steps in lieu of a tripod.

In a trice, fine residential houses—with nice people—

flanked the road which led to London's first sprawl into the open country, at Letchworth, where a garden village in fact gave each householder a garden to cultivate. How finely did this 1903 venture continue to prove with its Quaker inhabitants, who would allow no public houses to be built, nor would have washing exhibited on Sundays, for the garden system of planning extended to other areas with success. The village has grown to a town with a fine shopping centre, where I called to renew my liquid supply and travelled on.

The landscape stretched far into the limits of distant haze, yet in between, the huge motorway like the strings of a great double bass instrument gave off a long, incessant drone. Thank heaven I lost the roar, when my road slipped down into the charming village of Graveley with its dual duck-pond busy with noisy occupants. I sat in the bus shelter amongst some school children to scan my map, while the girl next to me did her homework as the others exchanged chatter until the bus came.

I had only to go 1½ miles into Stevenage, but with the ambiguity of the digs' address it proved to be treble that distance. Setting off hopefully to arrive before dark I saw three signs, North, West, and South Stevenage. I chose the nearest and found myself amongst new roads, with the sound of tearing monsters, in very fact there were two close at hand, one in the act of consuming a poor fellow whose head was completely swallowed. He was however making a battle of it, for his arm stretched out with a spanner about to be thrust in the beast's throat. The creature must have been yawning with indigestion, for out came the head of the bulldozer driver smeared with dragon's blood, and he yelled, "Where have you come from Mester?"

I told the driver, "North Scotland."

"What?" he said. "If I'd to go to t'corner shop, I'd get t'car out!"

We waved, and inside two minutes I found myself on the approach lane to the motorway.

Taxiing off with a full rucksack is difficult, so I kept speed down to a steady 3 m.p.h. and took the sinful liberty of keeping on the grass verge for a good mile, and then clambered up the banking looking for North Stevenage. Thank heavens at last, for with mountains of clay, soil and mud and no one to give me lucid direction I was lost. Hoisting the rucksack on a post I clambered over the fence and found myself with two curious horses in the field. I like horses, but not curious ones which have a nasty habit of offering pairs of muddy heels. I braved it across to the first building, a public house, which was closed and with a big barking dog on guard. The next, a posh bungalow, houses the nicest Irish woman you ever met. She gave me a cup of tea, got on the phone and rang the Austins to inform them I was on my way.

"Good evening lady, can you direct me to —— please?"

"Mister, where do you live?"

"Near Sheffield, madam."

It was enough. I thought she would have wept. She grasped my hand, "Oh, I'm from Rotherham. I'm ever so happy to have seen you, it's like being at home to hear you. Get in the car, I'll take you, wherever it is."

No: the Devil with all his wiles could not induce me to cheat not one inch, not with even a beautiful lady. "No, I must walk, but very many thanks." She looked very happy as the dusk swallowed her up and I struggled on until, with the most logical guidance I had received erstwhile, from a Pole, who in his broken English turned me into the very thoroughfare where Mr Austin—another peripatetic musician—came excitedly to greet me and in ten minutes I had the bath tap running.

Mrs Austin saw me out into the airy plains until eventually I was set fair for London and the south to make whatever progress I could before dark. An old lady seeing me asked my mission and so charmingly congratulated me on my achievement; had she seen me at the end of the same day I can well conjecture a different story. (Who said Southerners don't speak? They are just as nice as folk anywhere else, but really they have to be wary against the few vagabonds that are at large.)

The sky took on a true-to-type appearance for November—a leaden grey—accompanied by a clammy coolness. It made easier walking, as I forged on past large fields surely much favoured by visiting American cousins, for they must have been three-quarters of a mile across, but much to my delight, in the distance, some woods rose gently on the swelling earth, with here and there the peeping eyes of house windows. Some sporadic building showed one of the most handsome residential schemes I had seen. Soon the woods bordered the road where every style of modern building seemed to crane shoulders in an endeavour to be eyes that watched my progress; someone seemed as if she had, for as I sat down on a form to enjoy the view, a well-dressed, harassed looking woman came and poured out her soul to receive my sympathy. I listened and offered my condolences which would not relieve greatly her bitterness of spirit, for she had been 'brushed aside', and at a convenient moment I arose to go.

I was some way on towards the fine place of Old Welwyn before I stopped thinking of the sad woman and passed under the A1 and into the beautiful town. The old twisting roads with splendid buildings of antiquity and maintained so creditably made me wish to get clicking my camera for 'lecture shots', but the leaden sky began to leak a fine drizzle which stopped me using it. Still ambling about the busy main street and byways, folk seemed to be like the Chesterfield crowds with time to spare, and not too bothered if vehicles had to meander a zigzag course to make their journeys. Returning to look at the old church more thoroughly, I saw it had characteristic flint walls with stone quoins, and dark black–brown flints like cannon balls set in the white filigree of lime mortar made the edifice the town's best feature. Inside there had been tragedy when the choir was destroyed recently, but fortunately the screen was rescued and placed parallel with the nave which has proved to have bettered the acoustics. The wood carving is a delight and the balustrading superb as the shaping is twisted, a characteristic requiring great skill when hand turned.

Some ladies busy cleaning and generally beautifying the interior were so anxious I should miss nothing, and insisted I should also have a coffee, poured out in a beaker which had just been used. It was no use showing my reluctance but my stomach did not rebel as I drank, for church members often drink from the same sacramental vessel; there was tremendous goodwill in their gesture, I couldn't offend. The ladies then showed me an old thatch hook suspended under the eaves on an adjacent building, a relic of the days when it would be situated handier, when roof thatch catching alight from sparking wood fires could be raked off the roof until water was available. There would have been no thatch fire today, even so being the 5th, for the rain had set into a damp pall likely to last, so I sat in a garage and dined before setting out on my last lap before dark, having for the privilege of sheltering to send two cards from Dover to the garage attendants.

These fellows saw me out on that grim squelchy afternoon where, being beside the A1, murk from spinning tyres soon enveloped me in wet, cold, miserable mud from top to bottom; there was no dodging it, because of high banking to the footpath. I must have been the sorriest picture in Britain, and in no time had not one dry stitch on me; I even called at a house for a plastic bag to put my 'waterproof' watch in, and then pressed on. What had cost me a fortune was my 'waterproof' clothing, but this beneficent blessing of English weather ignored all standards of fairness and proved it to be a fallacious attribute of every garment.

At last reaching a public house, to ask for directions on this aquatic expedition, I could see every eye turn in my direction, and it takes something really unusual to detract many people from expensive thirst-quenching. I daren't sit down on the nice stools, nor lean against the counter, or stand steaming against the fire. I *flew* out, crossed the terrifying roundabout and went by Hatfield with a splish or splash from every step of my sodden boots.

Hatfield has its attractions in fair weather, but no one even thought of sightseeing for me in the incessant rain, so while being wet I decided to continue until dusk and called in at an A.A. box where two fine fellows let me dry my soggy cap, and share some steaming hot tea. They told me that on a right day there is some fine property to see, especially the Old Palace where Elizabeth I received news that through Mary her sister's death, accession to the throne was open to herself. Probably this weather was in remorse for that historical commemoration, or for the capture of Guy Fawkes, but probably for both as the day was so sorry for itself.

I left these men and continued into open country where

large fields divided by fences and fine trees would have been inviting enough to cross by their signposted footpaths, to the hamlets now piercing through the murk of low cloud. I sat under a flyover bridge and had my snack, resolved to call it a day when the first accommodation offered hospitality, and then set off. It could have been gorgeous for I trudged on by a tremendous length of an avenue of fine poplars, which gleamed like ice fairies in the beams of lorry headlights, now turning to a yellow mist from fog lamps searching the gloom. At last a transport house loomed out of the growing darkness and in I 'dived' asking, "Can you put me up for the night please?"

"No sir. Try next place farther on!"

I tried farther on with the same result, when a woman's kind eyes met mine, and seeing my predicament she then tried hard to arrange for success, but it was useless. Absolutely awful pouring rain and with nowhere habitable about, my only course was to continue to the first property or inn, and try again; how far I couldn't tell.

I crossed the side road just as a woman cyclist turned to go in the same direction as myself. She rode without lights on the footpath illuminated from the traffic's fog lamps. I followed on through the pools in the hollows, for the grass was just as sodden, until the woman disappeared. At length in North Mimms an inn's lights showed but no one answered my knocks—not six o'clock! I asked then at a door, in a row of old cottages when a female voice called "Who is there?"

"Will you kindly direct me to some hotel, please?"

The door opened slightly and then wider, when the woman asked, "Who are you? What are you doing out in this rain? Have you tried elsewhere? Are you retired? What was your job? What Committee? Do step inside, I will make you a meal, when you have dried your clothes or changed."

When we had dined together, Miss Shute, a retired teacher, asked me many more questions which in some cases had been asked before, and then said, "You may stay, Mr Kyme, if you would like the simple accommodation I can offer." I did, for no royal prince ever laid his head on a better pillow than I did in the makeshift conditions in the old house. Miss Shute had seen me before as I left the second transport house as she was about to cycle on the footpath; and checked and double-checked the truth of my statements before she would have me in. Honesty pays, I thought as I dried my sodden vest by the wood fire, and felt thankful for the spontaneous goodwill of a stranger.

29 *London*

THE murkiest night that ever fell on 5 November gave way to a brighter morning in North Mimms, and a jaunty gait soon had me passing picturesque old cottages and a stream.

Thank heavens within striking distance of the Metropolis there is a stream, where youngsters can paddle or fish for tiddlers, and where field paths and a golf course offer priceless freedom from the roar of traffic. A distant castle near some woodland looked like a German stronghold in the Black Forest, yet boundaries kept me from it, to the roadway where speed maniacs seemed hell-bent on getting into or out of London at lunatic speeds.

Turning off the main road towards Barnet for a bit of peace, I found this at Trotters Bottom, still unspoilt with fields and woods. The wind tugged at the last leaves on tall trees, so I went into an inn to warm up, the only customer. I was told that in this ancient parish a terrible plague affected the area in 1728, when a kind of smallpox doubled the death rate in a year. History was formed hereabouts, since inoculation was given experimentation on paupers, to see if such means of treatment could have bearing on curing sufferers from such a scourge.

Out into the cooler air thickening with fog, past allotments, tidy middle-class houses, shops, bigger shops, people, more people, jostling people—through into Barnet where 'begins the *north*', with its fine old church, and gibbet—gone. The gateway of hope to Dick Whittington and many more; and escape route for Dick Turpin some 300 years ago.

An air of prosperity lingers in Barnet, where long gardens were used to indicate the better status of house owners, and where each dwelling would support a housemaid; now with high claims on land, 'high'-reaching properties rake the sky, grey like the weather—concrete and glass.

Striding on, dodging here and there, forgetting the politeness I usually permit myself to use, or else progress would have been slow indeed, I finally threaded my way to a florist's counter. His question indicated how incongruous was my apparel in his place! "I say governor, where've you come from, a long way?——Listen——and he's walked all the way!" I suppose to the Londoner all kinds of appearances are commonplace, with folk of so many nationalities, and they don't warrant the raising of an eyebrow. However, for him to see me 'getting on a bit', with a huge haversack, anorak, red beret, red stockings, knee breeches, rounded heeled boots, stick, and a pot of flowers, must have caused a 'second look'.

For my reception at the Godgins, my Jewish friends, I could easily have thought that I had turned off from the Mall, by the Victoria Memorial, past the sentries, across the forecourt and into the Royal Household. No reception could have given me greater joy, and just like so many others, they gave me a wonderful chance to hear of their experiences and relax. What a difference to find a welcome, than to go to a place with sodden clothes and boots, shirt, vest, and wet skin, to be told, "No room 'ere, mister". "Can you tell me where please?" "No idea, mister", for the twenty-second time.

I learned much of our attitude to others and found the happiest folk were those who went to some trouble to meet a new situation with effort, irrespective of whether it would be gainful to them.

Sylvia Godgin packed me all sorts of good things and saw me off with Sam, who went with me towards the East End for company, I did not want to see the usual hackneyed things, but somewhere 'off beat' on a Sunday in this London, with no plane trees with peeling bark as at Hammersmith far west, where there are plenty. I recall one with full foliage one day, and none the next after a raid, the blast had ripped the leaves off, and one of my church friends too. She was killed, an old gentle lady—what had the tree, or she, done to deserve this?

In the same period I used to carry my drawing board over my head during the darkness of raids in 1940 to avoid shrapnel injury when returning from cancelled art classes. Almost got 'pinched'! This was a Sunday at Hammersmith Bridge where two soldiers were throwing bread in the air for gulls to retrieve. I took out my sketch block to draw the movements as the birds swooped with several similar actions, and replaced my book as the bread supplies ran out. I turned to go, when a police officer demanded, "Give me that book!"

"Why should I?"

"Never you mind, 'and it over."

"Why?" I demanded.

"BECAUSE I WANT IT——Where's the bridge, mate?"

"I haven't drawn the bridge!"

"Then what have you been drawing?"

I showed him the seagulls—"There, look!" He seemed disappointed. I never drew any more in London after that, only the deer in Richmond Park.

Sam Godgin had turned about as I ambled down through Upper Holloway, the place known to some unfortunate women who have suffered for principles not acceptable to the public of their day. Such a one was Mrs Pankhurst, 'Kept in' for three years, yet 'out' she evinced a great wit. She was addressing a meeting at Hathersage in Derbyshire when in a full hall a male heckler shouted, "Mrs Pankhurst, don't you wish you were a man?" She paused a moment looking at him directly and replied, "Yes—don't you?"

I sat and watched the empty streets and ate my meal, the place grey with stucco plastering, and dirty yellow-bricked dwellings with shabby fallpipes. I thought: What drab prospects of beauty are there here for folk who are ageing or too ill to go about? It seemed to me to be one big prison and I wished for these poor folk the joy of some plane trees and grass lawns. Yet I am told the days are done when a man must live near his work, and remain there when he can't afford to move.

Two women asked me to go into the Baptist church and have 'something warm inside', a typical gesture of these fine East Enders. Then on I went past John Wesley's statue, a fine monument which reminded me of Thomas Carlisle's in Chelsea, the finest piece of metal casting in London, which many people fail to visit. The patience used in doing such intricate and faultless work was amazing, and seems not less than when Carlisle, hearing J. S. Mill (a pompous visitor) had allowed by carelessness a maid to light a fire with his two-years' manuscript, had to *begin again.*

Continuing through back streets and forests of tall sky-scrapers, the strange odour from the waters pervaded the atmosphere with hypnotic effect; there is no smell on earth like the 'body' odour of Old Father Thames from about Hammersmith to the sea. It is different in the Cotswolds, with its little tributaries clean and sparkling, the place for children to go for outings. A teacher told me of one such trip when the youngsters paddled about, one lad seeming deeply involved on his own with mud and stones damming up the flow, until it virtually stopped. Satisfied, he stretched full height and said, "I wonder what they'll be doing in London now I've stopped the river?"

Can anyone leave the city without a backward glance at St Paul's, Big Ben and its bigger cousin the Shell-Mex clock?

How many more that late afternoon jostled my approach to see the Tower, mums and dads and wide-eyed youngsters milling about gaping in wonder. I thought of the old stone staircase to an upper apartment where tired sentries, 'nodding off' on guard, would not notice dangerous intruders, but for one thing, which would put them 'on the ready'. The stair-case has a long flight of evenly spaced steps, and near the top a much deeper one which breaks the rhythm and causes the unwary to stumble, bringing about their doom and that of their cause also.

I continued over the Tower Bridge where its two huge cantilevers meet, and stood athwart the joint with a youthful pleasure, like a colossus; then, like the tide beneath, I surged on to the south-east. Gone the mysterious patterns of lights reflected amongst the hulls and masts of floating craft, like so many golden candy sticks waving in some tribal ritual. Not even Venice could offer in this haunting twilight a more interesting canvas than this ancient waterway.

I was plunging into a part of London unknown to me, and felt friendless like the lonely folk in parks who feed and speak to sparrows to feel companionship, but the sparrows were now roosting, their day done, whilst I tried one place, five, ten places for accommodation with no fortune. I thought of the old woman I had seen sitting on some tavern steps, with an old pram loaded with her chattels. She was unkempt, grey haired, silently contemplating a frothy glass containing some ale, and still had some good fortune left.

My luck seemed to have run out for I tried hotels, public houses, and ordinary dwellings on this soggy November night, when two Irish folk, intellectual and generous, gave me refreshment, and told me to return if I couldn't get in. "We'll contrive something!" said P. E. Logan and his fiancée, as off I went into the grim night with interminable searching, until two kind old folk with a foot against the door held it ajar, scrutinized me from that distance, heard my story, and finally admitted me to arrange by phoning where someone could put me up. I was in, glad to stay amongst some friendly Germans staying in a Christian hostel under the supervision of the renowned Rev. Paul Oestreicher at Blackheath.

30 *To the Last Ditch*

THE foul misery of November weather last night gave way to scintillating sunshine and sparkling wet foliage this morning, and the grim-looking buildings of last night barricaded against intruders were revealed this morning to be mansions, one formerly occupied by General Wolfe of Quebec fame. No pathways to the sides of the Dover Road across the heath, I squelched through the sodden grass to avoid certain death from charging lorries and soon started with agonizing foot troubles. Wet feet cause blisters. A kind chemist gave me expert attention, and changing into dry hosiery I resolved to keep my boots dry by avoiding any foliage on wet days.

The autumn colours of wet leaves in the southern counties are superb and excelled themselves as I surged into Kent. Automobile dragons of every type roared in each direction with not one driver able to take leave of his task to see the beauty each side of the road. This was the Kent of London's overspill with nicely matured houses, not snooty ones. A greengrocer's van stood outside one where a woman with some children was making purchases, and as she looked kindly I asked if she would, when able, kindly fill my flask with water. "Come along sir, I will with pleasure"—which resulted in me being fêted as in Scotland.

Regaled, I sped on, not over the Kent as flat as a billiard table, but along the undulating road between high hedges. I could well imagine the same track a couple of centuries before, narrower, pot-holed, gravelled, coppice-lined, offering hides for poor fellows without jobs marauding to keep alive; or of others, avaricious malefactors who would kill if need be to gain some loot.

Had not Dickens passed this way often by coach, inside, or on the board according to the weather? His sharp eye would gather useful information about any interesting wayfarers in a moment, to be stored in his mental library for future literary use. It did occur to me that had our paths crossed, it would have been a challenge to his pen. After two months of weather my face was the colour of leather, offset by long, grey sideburns (radar scanners). My apparel had lost every trace of newness from my anorak down to my crinkled boots. The square-handled ash-plant stick had been a godsend to relieve my arthritic knee, and the great bulk of the blue rucksack, pocketed, laced and buckled, had harboured all kinds of indispensable mysteries.

When having caught him up at the inn, he would likely have asked, "What the 'Dickens' do you carry all that lot for?" as I slowly revealed the items for other lone travellers to see. First, out of one pocket would come the pint flask contained in a stout-walled plastic container, to safeguard against breakage and any spilled liquid seriously damaging photographic equipment and materials. The second pocket—a plastic box for food; and one in the third for letters, testament, maps and notebooks.

On a number of occasions, my precious photographic records would have been ruined but for plastic bags which had the tops twirled around and secured by thin twisted wire. Similarly all changes of clothing were bone dry by using suitable plastic envelopes.

"What's this here?"

"Dickens, that's half a tooth brush, I cut off much of the handle to save carrying unnecessary weight 800 miles."

"What's the main thing you've found out about effective walking?"

"Keep feet dry and have plenty of extra socks; incidentally I found a pair on each shoulder effectively prevents shoulder straps from chafing—particularly in hot weather."

As the beauties of autumn hedgerow foliage gave way to distant panoramas of farmlands, signs of the great ravages of bulldozers came in view as gigantic wedges cut out of the landscape of woodland hills allowed traffic to roar ahead on straight roads. I felt uneasy as traffic surged past unpleasantly near, stirring up clouds of paper and dust—I was on a motorway. My map did not include this modern innovation and there was no one to ask how to get off. To see a village for location was impossible, the banking was so high. I'll risk it and keep going, I thought, and make as many miles as possible before leaving it. I felt like a usurper paying no road tax speeding at $3\frac{1}{2}$ m.p.h. when, *Honk, honk: "Will the walker on the down road to Dover leave the road at once"*—spat out on the air from a fast car, with a police-capped officer glowering from the nearside window in my direction. I felt my ears burning, but spurned my cowardice, and since the juggernaut was gone in a cloud of dust I continued. Going at a fast rate my misdemeanour slipped my conscience until, *Honk, honk,* etc. The car pulled up in the off lane, but traffic prevented the officers rushing across, which gave me a chance to mount the banking faster than any 'Olympic time', to hide myself in the hedgerows until police radio trekkers would not hope to find me.

Finding excellent accommodation near Dartford through the kindly efforts of a car driver who returned to tell me he had found a place, I settled in, thankfully before dark, and wrote up my notes.

Tuesday, nice and cool and off like a lark to a high plateau on which were a number of modern factories, including the giant concern of Bowaters paper factory; and then into the vast beyond of spreading spaces.

A flash of brilliant whiteness dazzling to the eyes came and was gone, followed by repetitions, and peering through hawthorn hedges, a tremendous quarry revealed its huge faces and platforms on which it appeared Dinky-like toys were scooping up and conveying loads of chalk. They seemed so small compared with the huge crater they were working in. Three sizeable villages could have been lost on top of each other, in that yawning chasm from which all the world's supplies of teachers' chalks and Bowaters paper fillers for a thousand millenniums may have been taken. I wanted to sculpt a huge Churchillian profile on a giant façade, yet one thing at a time kept me to my purpose as the high chalk hills plummetted down again and took me into the grey chilly November wind, my only company lorries and more lorries. I thought, if only I could escape these vehicles.

A wayside transport café with steamy windows offered warmth of hot soup and more coffee, and unable to resist these temptations, I dived in. Asking a pleasant attendant what I could find of interest off the main road on a parallel south-eastwards, he asked, "Don't you know these parts? Don't you know Cobham and Dickens' Leather Bottle Inn?" Warmed up, I was off like a hare into the glorious lanes of Kent and across some fields into Cobham, amongst a huddle of oast houses, seemingly gathered to keep warm from the chill wind over the fields of stubble. Cooing doves sat on a cross-member inside an oast cowl sheltering from the cold with unruffled feathers, half drunk probably from hop odours from below; and from the clutter of high hedges fencing old gardens, I emerged to see the old church.

A dual choice faced me—the church or the Leather Bottle first? Here were two fine old places known to Dickens and as like when he knew them, save that shocking 'no parking' lines spoiled the old road. (Could not sign boards a quarter of a mile from each entry stating 'No parking beyond here' save such desecration of this otherwise perfect example of old world England?)

Old trees surrounding the church stood starkly against the fitful sky, matched in grim silhouettes by the gravestones about which I sauntered. How many names did the celebrated author use from such sources? An old charming pair, the Gerrishes, turned over a page of their history for me and gave an answer. Here along the old gritty road many a waggonette rattled along after the sharp crack of the whip, taking home to Gillingham and Rochester the sightseers after a day's outing in the surrounding picnic fields, the village, the Leather Bottle, and the church. They said how to this ancient hostelry of rustic brick and half timbering, with its swinging sign of Dickensian character, many celebrated people have called and added their names in the invaluable visitors' book, namely of royalty, nobility and members of the illustrious acting fraternity. I went in to confirm the sight of this cosy old place decorated with pictures depicting many scenes from the author's novels. It seemed a hallowed place, this very room where he penned his *Pickwick Papers*; and no stretch of my imagination was needed to see amongst the tobacco smoke the characters hereabouts he could have drawn. Oh yes, Snodgrass! He found that name as he strolled round the graveyard, and to look more keenly one would undoubtedly find more names of characters.

I left Mr and Mrs Gerrish to wander down the memory lane of Cobham, and struck out down leaf-covered lanes past a herd of donkeys marked with their crosses indicative of our Lord's kingly ride towards his crucifixion. They seemed lonely, and I privileged one by rubbing his nose. In a trice I was in Rochester to stay the night.

Weather again superb, a good thing! Soon crossed the Medway broad and gleaming like a Venetian lagoon, seeing afloat all manner of craft, and buildings of variety flanking its banks; all every bit as exciting as the Italian queen of cities. It was superb, and I eulogized on the scene with a lady who answered my salutation with "Goot morning."

"From Germany, are you?"

"Yesss."

She seemed pleased with my limited attempt to say it was beautiful—"Zehr gutte."

"Yah!" I told her she must see the old castle which would remind her of her homeland; the Bull tavern, and others, made famous by Dickens' writings; the Bishop's Yard, and finally the magnificent cathedral.

Forgive my audacity, I again furtively trespassed to see a forbidden sight, I simply hadn't the time to go and disturb someone for permission; it was like Eve's apple—fabulous.

I walked through a side door into the cathedral where boys were leaving their school service to the accompaniment of magnificent organ music. Some of us stood to listen to the varying tone and volume, swelling at last to voluminous triumph—an offering of praise. The echoes receded and then I asked what great organist had officiated this morning. "It's a schoolboy, sir," and glad I was to congratulate young David Poulter, sixteen, one of a number of young people who work on a roster for playing at morning worship.

The cathedral is a feast of architectural splendour, with window-glass rich in colour giving an ethereal glow over the whole building. A huge nave is supported by massive pillars of varying sections with linking arches finely ornate with masonic carvings. Yet of all this masterpiece's wonders is the stone altar panel, to me as moving a sight as the 'Last Supper' by Leonardo da Vinci. Undoubtedly Rochester Cathedral was my greatest architectural surprise on route.

Near Chatham, quaint and beautiful—so different from my own conjectures, with steep streets and a fine memorial to the fallen high on a hill top, I sat on a form for a snack in the warm sunshine, and watched a red admiral butterfly sun itself for ten minutes before flying off—no end to the pleasant surprises of the south.

I stood at a clock-tower memorial given by the Japanese years ago, in memory of a fine Englishman who, when he was shipwrecked on a foreign shore, served his adopted country with enthusiasm. Even yet do the Japanese send yearly a representative of their nation to pay tribute to this remarkable man, William Adams 1524-1612, formerly of the Elizabethan fleet, who taught his adopted countrymen maths, geography, and ship designing.

On into the country of Roland Hilder, of oast-houses, hop-poles, apple orchards, farms and barns; it was most enjoyable. I found pleasure in pacing out the distance between the immaculate rows of poles leaving enough room for trestles to be moved, and thought of 'circus men' on stilts fixing the wires from pole tops. There was a beauty of its own in the gaunt timbers and wires; of bare fruit trees; gone were the blossoms, and the hampers, and baskets of colourful fruit; no more the chatter of birds stealing cherries.

Now the cavalcades of lorries were intermittent, and in the lulls the quietness of winter reigned; no twittering birds sounded from the empty nests in the stark hedgerows surveyed solemnly by the gaunt, defunct oast-house. This was the peaceful county, of cricket and Canterbury, the gateway to pilgrims to and from this country. How different in the early 'forties when planes of one sort and another soared high enough, or hedge-hopped low enough, to avoid trouble. What county suffered more the alarms, annoyance, discomfort and distress than valiant Kent during air raids? It was not unlike Leonardo da Vinci who, hearing the battle a few fields away, continued his artistic project; life or death, 'it must go on', so did the folk of Kent continue their wartime projects, even bearing the hell of doodlebugs.

Still continuing and making enquiries for 'digs', a lady

replied at the end of a village, "Sorry, sir, I've a large family, but rest and have tea with us." I had my own food and talked with her husband and family. The breadwinner was a farm worker who, to augment income, repaired cycles. He jumped up from his meal twice to deal with clients—a happy man, and like his wife and boys nice to meet, who gave me a fillip to round off my longest stint of twenty miles. Luckily I had an excellent address in distant Faversham.

Wet or fine, day or night, Faversham is a delight for the artist, with gleaming streets reflecting the small-paned windows and half-timbered buildings with their quaint gables. This conglomeration of twisting streets is, with Rochester, also the reminder of olden times.

An acquaintance of mine on holiday returned home near Faversham during war-time, and, since travel was limited, he wandered around the farmlands, where on one gate it stated, 'Honey for sale'. He asked, "May I have two jars please? I hope you don't think I'm greedy."

"Oh no, you can have more if you wish," he was told.

Getting home with his precious good find, he had been 'stung', for the bees had been busy amongst onion flowers—'the proof is in the eating'.

I had made good progress towards Canterbury in the scintillating splendour of a sunny morning, with hanging twigs bejewelled with heavy moisture, when a fellow from a nearby field chatted with me about his job. He wanted companionship, so put down his muddy tools and leaned on the fence and discussed problems attached to hop growing. "Yes, we use chestnut timber for poles, and by the way, you've heard of chespoles for fencing? You see, chestnut doesn't rot so easily as other woods and doesn't need much attention; and your question about only creosoting about a foot of each pole above ground; we don't let the creosote touch the ground to avoid poisoning plant life. The butt of a pole in the ground is always moist and doesn't decay, it's the part just above which would become alternately wet and dry which would soon rot, so we treat enough to prevent it getting ground dampness to save trouble."

We said "Adieu" and parted, and as I climbed the steep slope I turned to watch him digging the soggy ground and to my joy saw the *sea* again! The first time from Solway Firth. What beautiful homes graced that hillside with such a delectable view! I could readily have made Kent my home county. Soon the unmistakable cathedral towering above the clean town with its great stone gateways drew me yet again into its mellowed interior, and even in November it still had its visitors of all races viewing the many historic features of this noble edifice.

I recall once photographing the interior very early, and was politely asked to discontinue in that area until after prayers. "Would you care to join us sir?" I did, and made up a company of seven praying for the peace and blessing of our country—a service I will never forget.

I still found something new and compared the wonder of the tablet showing the 'Good Samaritan' with that in Bath Abbey, indicative of the skill that draws men's attention to our great buildings. I felt cut down to scale as I emerged from the seat of Christendom to continue my penultimate trek, and was soon out of town between high hedges. The sun low, heralded approaching dusk, and for the last time in over sixty days I looked for accommodation, in Bridge. Yet again, two good souls allowed me to sleep on a settee after having written a shoal of postcards for posting on the morrow, which soon came—mistily—as I took to the old Roman road.

Still undulating, the old road fought its way between huge deciduous trees, until reaching high chalk downs enveloped in greyness, the clammy coldness and marrow searching wind kept me resolutely to my task. No one, no animal or bird, could I see on those wide plains of desolate farmlands as the cold European air drifted by me, and but for occasional lorries I could well have been in the greyness of Ayrshire for I had not spoken to a soul all morning.

Some feeling of a Canterbury pilgrim heading for sacred Jerusalem struck me, as the long stretch before me twisted about following easier contours, when a milestone indicating 'DOVER 10 miles' appealed to me as a suitable place for my last meal and a delayed-action photograph of myself. That record over, the metaphorical dust from my heels flew, until in the distance the rhythmic music of chopping coming from a large shed near a house caused me to call in at the open door. It seemed again like Scourie, with the reek of a woodworker's craft. Outside in neat piles stood sharpened hedge-stakes yellow with newness, all a length, as neat as a sheet of pins. Here and there were rolled up lengths of chespoles wired up ready to put round the finest park of any dukedom. I stood and looked in awe at the tidiness of offcuts and choppings ready to sell for firewood, when a soft, kind voice spoke as the chopping ceased. I congratulated the man—about my age—who delighted in such tidiness and immediately a comradeship sprang up, since we both knew the same medium, odours, and feel the same thrill of manipulation with a sharpened tool, and ease in labour with a keen edge, or for that matter the same danger with inattention. We both knew the same satisfaction of a door well made, or a pile of new stakes for a Kentish farmer—"No, I wouldn't change my life for factory work for all the wealth in the world," he said as he took up his axe to the sound of fading rhythm.

A fine sweep of a steep slope slipped into Lydden where André, the publican of the Hope Inn, beneficently regaled me with bitter lemon before my last fling, when off I went, more in reverie than any sight-seeing. Lost in thoughts of God's care for me, the folk I had met, the wonders I'd seen, when my eye caught the sight of frantic waving hands from a car over the road. Press folk? Never! Two ladies wanted me to cross over.

"Good afternoon, madam," I said to the older one, "can I help you?"

"Don't you know me?" she pleaded.

Looking hard, I replied, "Lady, I've seen so many nice folk on this long journey, I just can't recall where."

"Badcall!"

"Of course, you kindly gave me a drink that hot afternoon near Scourie—small world."

Mrs Weir had looked for days hoping to see me, and her and her daughter's greeting made light my last miles into the misty conglomeration of houses and traffic where I mixed with little throngs, one reverently paying tribute to the fallen of many forces, by placing poppies on the memorial tableau; it was 12 November.

I was proud to have finished my venture in Dover, the

blunt 'chin' of Britain. This bulwark, washed by the Channel waters once 'worth a bob a gallon' to keep the enemy at bay, is the place where men and women defiantly showed unbelievable courage to do their part for freedom. This is the place where an ageing woman would not leave her house in the worst of the war, so that she could offer welcome drinks to forces personnel in an atmosphere of home.

I had one thing to do and crossed the promenade, deserted but for two lads with fishing lines confidently searching the dark, soughing waters beyond the rails for bites. I found a space to the gravelly beach and inched my way to the gently lapping white edges of the surf and dipped my hand, *our* mission fulfilled, for on so many others had the venture depended.

A peaked-capped, uniformed fellow accompanied me towards the station, and wondered by my appearance what I had been up to, when I asked if he would care to contribute one item to the book's conclusion. He couldn't. "Where were you in the wartime?" I asked, and Petty Officer Whitwall of hovercraft navigation said how he was, as a small boy, removed from his home in Dover to safer quarters in Canterbury. There he 'fell from the frying pan into the fire', for one night the enemy bombed the cathedral city so terrifyingly that young Whitwall removed the large key from the kitchen door lock in order to see for himself how the fires raged, yet looked on undaunted.

"Derek," I said, "That's it; you had a keyhole picture of war." And, if you have read thus far, you have had a keyhole picture of experiences in a no more exciting 800-mile walk in this world.

Incidentally, do join me on my next journey.

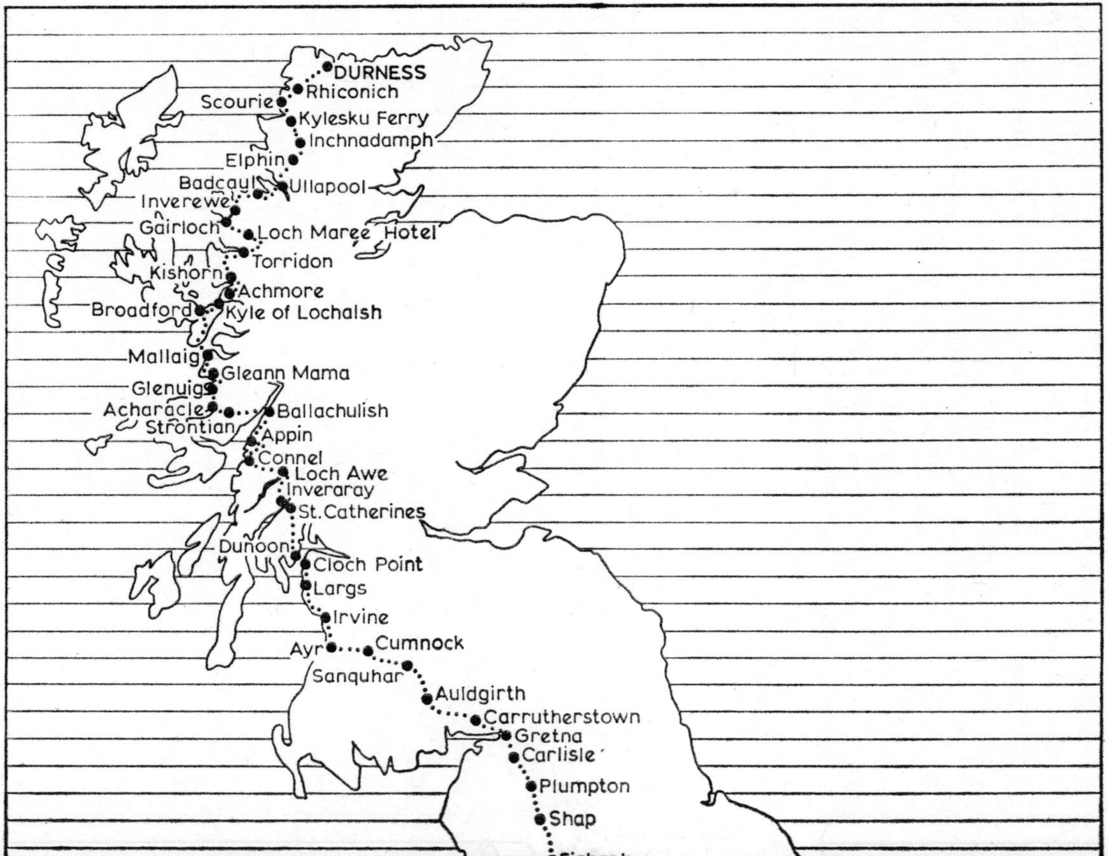
DURNESS
Rhiconich
Scourie
Kylesku Ferry
Inchnadamph
Elphin
Badcaul
Ullapool
Inverewe
Gairloch
Loch Maree Hotel
Torridon
Kishorn
Achmore
Broadford
Kyle of Lochalsh
Mallaig
Gleann Mama
Glenuig
Acharacle
Ballachulish
Strontian
Appin
Connel
Loch Awe
Inveraray
St. Catherines
Dunoon
Cloch Point
Largs
Irvine
Ayr
Cumnock
Sanquhar
Auldgirth
Carrutherstown
Gretna
Carlisle
Plumpton
Shap

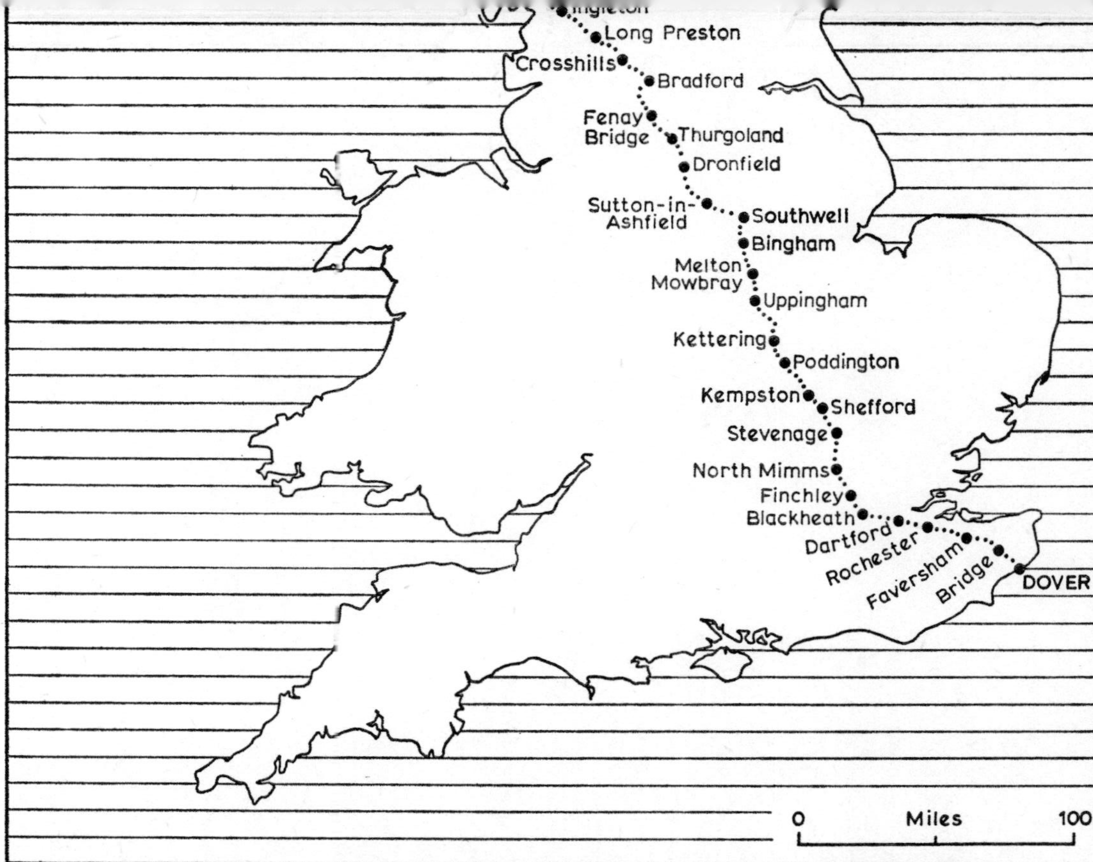
Long Preston
Crosshills
Bradford
Fenay Bridge
Thurgoland
Dronfield
Sutton-in-Ashfield
Southwell
Bingham
Melton Mowbray
Uppingham
Kettering
Poddington
Kempston
Shefford
Stevenage
North Mimms
Finchley
Blackheath
Dartford
Rochester
Faversham
Bridge
DOVER
0
Miles
100

Index

Index